Getting Published

A Guide for Businesspeople and Other Professionals

Gary S. Belkin

The Wiley Press
John Wiley & Sons, Inc.
New York   Chichester   Brisbane   Toronto   Singapore

Library of Congress Cataloging in Publication Data

Belkin, Gary S.
    Getting Published.
    Includes index.
    1. Authorship.   I. Title   II. Series: Self-teaching guide.

PN146.B44 1984   808'.02   83-6924
ISBN 0-471-89338-2 (pbk.)
0-471-88307-7 (cloth)

Acknowledgments

No book evolves in a vacuum and none is developed without the practical assistance and guidance of colleagues, friends, and other writers whose support and insight are integral to a book.

The initial impetus for this book was Dean Victor Marrow who encouraged me to offer continuing education workshops for professionals trying to publish, Dr. Andrew Robinson of Hunter College provided me with the opportunity to develop further these workshops with a most enthusiastic and motivated faculty. My editor at John Wiley, Alicia Conklin, gave form and direction to my original proposals, directing the inchoate intention of a well-meant project into the shape of a book. From proposal to galleys, her insight and intelligence provided a valuable beacon of direction. To her goes more than a mark of gratitude.

I also want to thank Barbara Charton, research librarian at Long Island University, whose reserves of patience and knowledge allowed me to fully appreciate the value of the Dialog information system (discussed in chapter 5) and who on innumerable occasions led me to the right place to find the special piece of information needed.

I owe a special debt of thanks to those great teachers who, over the years, helped me learn to write and gave me the encouragement to pursue writing as a profession: especially, Dr. Kenneth Bernard; Dr. Maxine Greene of Teachers College; Dr. Hildreth Kritzer; the late Dr. Samuel Tennenbaum; Dr. Martin Tucker.

Table of Contents

FOR JORDAN BELKIN

Introduction

If you fall into any of the following categories and have been thinking about writing, this book can help you achieve your goal.

- If you are a business or professional person – an attorney, physician, consultant, psychologist, academic, business executive, teacher, programmer, or accountant – who wants to communicate some of your innovative ideas, programs, or practices to other professionals or to the general public through the medium of print.
- If you are a person who possesses some expertise or unique insight in a specialized professional area (from computers to taxidermy) and wants to share your knowledge and experience with people who are interested in learning about the field.
- If you are an academician, scholar, researcher, or scientist hoping to publish your ideas in the professional journals – in areas ranging from police work to teaching to nuclear physics.
- If you are a graduate student working on a thesis or dissertation.
- If you are a teacher or other person with subject-matter expertise who wants to write a textbook for use in elementary, high school, or college courses.

In the following pages, I will concentrate on all practical aspects of getting professional work published, from making the initial decision about the most appropriate form in which to work (scholarly article, general magazine or trade journal article, text book, trade book, or professional–scholarly book), to increasing a book's sales after publication. You will also find detailed coverage on preparing introductory correspondence about your work for prospective publishers, how to find an agent and how to see that the agent works for you, as well as step-by-step procedures for developing the proposal for a book-length project, and a thorough discussion of the research, writing and reviewing stages of publication.

In addition to providing an overview about the many opportunities for publication and offering detailed information about the latest use of word processing and electronic technology in the development of a manuscript, *Getting Published* also introduces you to some effective writing methods that have been tested and proved successful in the seminars I have conducted at universities and professional organizations. The method of "writing in chunks" helps writers churn out pages and pages of good draft material without the enervating strain of composing a long, continuous first draft. The "three-page method" helps you expand a structured three-page exercise step-by-step into a finished article- or book-length work. Using these methods, many frustrated writers who have been struggling for years with their papers, books, or dissertations finally got their work off the ground, out of the planning and research stages, and into manuscript form – in the shortest amount of time. Follow these exercises carefully, as they are described in chapter 3, and they will also work for you.

Chapter 1, "The Opportunities for Professional Publication," offers a broad survey of the many ways a person can go about publishing his or her ideas, with the limitations and advantages of each approach. It shows how ideas begin to shape into a project as the prospective writer answers a few key questions. Chapter 2, "Developing Your Project," focuses in on this transformation from idea to development in terms of three basic phases: (1) defining the scope of your project and its market (audience); (2) allocating time for your initial research and your correspondence or proposal writing; and (3) reassessing the project before working on it by using feedback from editors and reviewers.

You get right down to the fundamentals of putting the plan into action in chapter 3, "Getting It On Paper." This chapter sets out five stages of successful writing endeavors, based on the actual problems prospective authors encounter, with examples from various professions and various target audiences and markets. The five stages are: (1) overcoming procrastination; (2) setting up a regular working schedule; (3) writing in chunks; (4) constructively using reviewers' feedback as you go along; and (5) bibliographic, reference, and permission file management. In this chapter you will also learn about the "three-page method," which reduces the resistance to writing that bogs down many potential projects.

Chapter 4, "Finding a Publisher," covers what for many authors is the single greatest deterrent to success–the belief that, "No one will ever publish what I have to say." You'll learn the answer to some basic questions. What does an agent or editor look for in a prospective author's query? How can you make your proposal most effective in terms of stating the uniqueness and advantages of your project? How can a proposal be used through the development of a book manuscript or a lengthy project? This chapter covers the question of how an author can sell his or her idea to the publisher.

Chapter 5, "Making Technology Work for You," covers an exciting new area for writers: applications of the new microcomputer and word processing technology to the craft of writing. Years ago, the typical academic or professional writer would spend hours poring over dusty journals on library shelves, copying pages of notes by hand, and finally spending a year or two sitting with quill in hand (later, at a manual typewriter, then an electric) and composing the work. But that was in the olden days.

In the 1980s, most successful writers use their time far more effectively. They search the literature through computer terminals that can also generate graphics to enliven the article or book. The actual writing process is facilitated on word processors that allow rapid composing and revision, as well as magnetic storage of reusable material. One of the prime goals of *Getting Published* is to show the prospective writer author that this type of equipment can now be used by almost all professional writers, in all stages of preparation from writing the intial correspondence to the publisher up through the index for a completed book.

When the writing of a draft is completed, the author's work is often halted by doubt and trepidation. In fact, this is a particularly crucial stage, where valid critical feedback from editors and reviewers can help the author make the strongest possible showing in the final product. In chapter 6, "Effective Strategies," we discuss this phase of preparation, along with a variety of writing "tricks" that have been effectively used by writers who have produced successful works.

There is no substitute for experience, certainly not in this field. Where can we better learn the ins and outs of professional publishing than from those who have been most successful at it? They have seen it all–from the inside. Chapter 7, "Some Advice from Professional Writers and Editors," poses some typical questions that are frequently asked by people thinking of writing for publication. These questions are put to some of the leading editors and writers of professional books and journals in the United States today.

The two appendixes offer some useful information to put into practice what you have learned throughout this book. Appendix A, "Where To Send Your Material," offers a list of professional publishers, with the kinds of books and journals they publish (their level and subject matter), their general policy, and to whom you should send your material. Appendix B, "Preparing Your Manuscript and Ancillaries," suggests some specific guidelines for preparing the proposal, manuscript, ancillary materials, and index in a physical format acceptable to publishers.

1

The Opportunities for Publication

When the jury came in with the verdict, John looked at his client proudly, for he knew that the judgment he had won for her might make legal history. Only three years out of law school, he thought it might be a good idea to write about this highly unusual case, not only to let other lawyers know about it, but also to get his name mentioned in this burgeoning field of product liability law. Within weeks after the decision, he started to write his article on the weekends and at night, and after three months of steady work, it was done. He sent it out to an excellent law journal, one that he personally enjoyed reading, and waited eagerly for their letter of acceptance.

Two months later, when John's article was rejected by the prestigious journal with a polite printed note, he took it in stride. "I guess I'm just not cut out to be a writer," he told his wife, and placed his twenty-two page manuscript in the junk drawer of his old desk. It never occurred to him that the problem was not his article, but rather where he had sent it. He did not realize that he had submitted it to the wrong journal, and that it was a good article and he should send it out again. So, like many aspiring writers who don't understand why some things get published and some do not, John's worthy work never saw print because he failed to follow a few basic rules about where to send an article or book idea.

Liz had been working for a year and a half on her book, writing weekends and summers, when she wasn't teaching. When friends asked about her work, she told them her book would be the most practical, the most interesting, the *best* book around on teaching methods for elementary school teachers, since she based it on her ten years of teaching experience. No boring theories and silly references like those fat dull books she had to read in her college education courses. One reader, a friend of hers, commented on how interesting her examples were, how lively the book was to read. Another reader, her sister's friend, assured Liz that she would have no trouble getting it published. The comments were always encouraging, so Liz kept pushing herself, fueled by the delicious fantasy that her book would be the best selling textbook on teaching in the country.

When Liz finally finished her manuscript – or got to the point where she thought eager publishers could begin bidding on it – she packed up the four hundred pages and sent them to a publishing house that was known for its many leading texts in education. That publisher returned it, with a brief letter that assured Liz it was not the quality of her manuscript they were rejecting but that "it just doesn't fit in with our present publishing plans." Undaunted, she sent it out to another publisher, then another . . . and then another. Each sent back a short polite letter saying about the same thing: Liz's book just didn't fit into their publishing plans. The seventh publisher remarked that Liz's book was of "excellent merit" and they were sure she would "find a suitable publisher." "Excellent merit!" Liz mused, reading the phrase over and over again. That was all she had to hear. And so, off went the five-and-a-half pounds of manuscript again, from one publisher to another, until Liz exhausted much of her funds on postage and copying, and her patience on waiting for the mailman. Finally, Liz, like many an aspiring writer, shelved the book and started going out weekends again.

A number of Pamela's colleagues and clients had been telling her she should write an article, maybe for the *New York Times* real estate section or for one of the local papers in her area, where the real estate ads were listed. "You know so much about buying a house, about what to look for," one client told her, "if you would only write it up, I'm sure thousands of people would want to read it." Another client told her that none of the articles he had been reading about how to choose the right neighborhood and what to look for in a new house was nearly as thorough or clear as the information Pamela had been giving him. "Why don't you write a book?" he asked her, and mentioned that his uncle was a big name in publishing.

A year later, colleagues and clients were still urging Pamela to put some of her ideas on paper. "I really should," she explained, "and I do intend to. But I've been so busy these past few months, I haven't had a second. Literally, not a second." But secretly Pam told herself, as she had done weekly for the past two years, that next week she would sit down and begin writing that article. Yes, she was ready. When she picked up the *Times* each Sunday, she had a little stirring of how nice it would be to see her article in section eight. But then something always came up and . . . well, you know how it is.

John, Liz, and Pamela are typical examples of people who want to publish but cannot because they don't understand how and why things get published or because they can't sit down and get their ideas on paper.

John and Liz have something interesting to write about, both have the ability to write, and – most importantly – both have actually taken the time to get it on paper. Yet, both remain unpublished.

Liz's problem, like John's was that she didn't know the market for which she was writing. John thought he was writing for a very scholarly law journal, but actually geared his article to a general law audience. Liz thought she was writing a textbook but she wasn't. What she was doing, in fact, was the very opposite of textbook writing: she was creating something completely different from what existed in the field, something that was not typically used in courses, something that represented her own point of view, not a general overview of an area.

Pamela's problem, just as common, was the malaise of procrastination. How many of us have in our minds a list of things we will do when we have the time? For those who want to write, writing is usually at the top of such a list – and remains there forever, as day after day passes by without the first word appearing on paper. Pamela felt the project so overwhelming, so far removed from her daily activity, that she couldn't get herself started on it.

These problems are typical of the pitfalls that trip many an aspiring writer. And yet, they can easily be avoided with the right information and the appropriate strategies toward publication possibilities.

Avoiding Common Pitfalls

If only John and Liz had known the realities of publishing life, they would have had an excellent chance of seeing their work in print. Two things that would have made a difference for them are these principles:

1. Always understand the audience (market) for whom you are writing.

2. Don't be discouraged by rejections – not by one, not by twenty, not by fifty. Many highly successful books and articles were published after a large number of rejections.

These are two of several reasons why people don't get their work published. But by the time you finish this book, they will no longer be problems for you. For in this and the following chapters, you will learn how to identify your market, how to gear your project for the market you choose, and how to use rejections and criticism constructively in working on your project.

There may be other reasons – just as relevant – that explain why you haven't had your work published. Perhaps you feel you don't have anything of great consequence to say.

When Dr. Porter, an adjunct faculty member at a small college, applied for promotion to associate professor, he was turned down because he hadn't published anything. He shrugged it off as just his due. "I don't really have anything that valuable to say," he admitted. What he didn't realize is that even if he only just tapped the surface of his twenty years experience as a health education teacher, he would find dozens of interesting things to say – things that he probably says all the time to his colleagues and friends, but which he doesn't think are important enough for publication.

If he only took an hour or two to thumb through some journals he would find that many of the things published there are no more profound or revolutionary than his ideas. In fact, most of the pages of print that fill the periodicals and the books of our libraries are by people just like you and me, writing about subjects and ideas that they have culled from their experiences. The John Deweys, Edmund Wilsons, and William Jameses are the exceptions, not the rule, in professional publication.

Yet many suitable candidates for publication are deterred from even trying to publish by the belief that they have nothing important to say. It is based on the myth that anything in print must be important. I call this resistance to getting things written the "mystique of the printed page," and this, probably more than any other reason, holds people back from even trying to publish. Once you overcome this – once you realize that you do have something to say – it is a short step to getting a project started with enthusiasm and belief in your own abilities.

EXERCISE

This little exercise has worked well for those who are overly impressed by the mystique of the printed page. Take your favorite journal and open to the beginning of any article. With a pen and paper, hand copy the first two paragraphs of the article. Read it over in your own handwriting and see if it looks different to you. Then, with a different color pen, make at least two corrections to improve some sentence or make some idea more interesting or concrete. Or, add a sentence or example. You will see that not only can you write the sort of thing that gets printed, but you can even improve upon it.

Other people have a different problem. They believe their ideas are valuable, but don't consider their writing abilities sufficient for publication. George, for instance, is a computer scientist. His colleagues at the laboratory have been encouraging him for years to write up his new ideas about designing simpler circuits in home computers before someone else does. But George is afraid to try because he doesn't feel he's a good enough writer to get his ideas across. Even in college he loved working with his hands in the lab, but hated writing up his results for his professors. He is overwhelmed by the task of getting started on a new article – terrified by the blank page in the typewriter and by his own feelings of clumsiness with words.

What he doesn't realize is that you can always find editorial assistance for the task of writing and that you need only organize your ideas and put them down on paper as you might speak into a tape recorder in order to get them to the point where an editorial advisor or writing assistant can help. We look later in this book at a method called "writing in chunks" and at the "three-page method," both of which can help you get your ideas down on paper with the least possible strain.

So far, we have seen four reasons that deter fully capable professionals from seeing their ideas published in journals or as books.

1. They don't understand the market.
2. They give up after a couple of rejections.
3. They think they don't have anything important to say.
4. They don't think they can write well enough to get published.

We will discover other reasons along the way, but for now it is a good idea to keep those four in mind as you begin to develop your own plan of what you want to write, where you want to have it published, and what effect you want it to have on your professional recognition.

You might want to think through what you will actually gain from writing – in terms of career growth, economic rewards, professional recognition and personal self-esteem. Then you will be in a better position to evaluate whether the effort of writing will be commensurate with the likely rewards.

The most typical reward is personal and professional recognition and self-esteem. What more satisfying feeling is there than to see one's ideas in print, to have one's family and colleagues praise one's work, to be able to hand out reprints of one's published article to a potential client? What greater thrill is there than to casually place a copy of your book on the coffee table, just close enough to be noticed but far enough away to be modest?

If, like some professionals, you are writing for money – beware. While the occasional million can be made from publishing, it is rare indeed to make even enough money to have justified the hourly labor. Few books become bestsellers and most of the journals and magazines to which you will be sending your material pay very little, if anything. And it is not always as easy to translate your written project into economic gain as you may think. Many consultants believe that if they have published a book, even a modest work, their fees can double and their workload will triple. While it is true that a published book or article bolsters one's credibility – and makes one's words more authoritative – don't expect miracles: there are just too many other published business and professional people competing in the marketplace.

So, what you end up with is a realistic perspective: that you will enjoy some rewards of professional recognition and self-esteem, but that you should not expect a publication or two to cause miraculous changes in your life or your career.

Evaluating Your Opportunities

What are some of the opportunities for professional publication? Where can you get your work published? How do you go about getting started?

The publication market is much larger than you probably realize. There are well over three thousand scholarly, professional, and technical journals. There are five times that many in-house journals, newsletters, and other sources of disseminating news to specialized audiences. While most of these do not pay for articles, there are hundreds of popular magazines, and over a thousand publishers of book-length work that do pay. There are publishers who specialize in everything from homosexuality to gourmet cooking to flying saucers.

First, you have to decide on the length of your project – book-length or article-length. If this will be your first effort at publication, it is probably wiser to think in terms of article-length publication for three reasons: (1) it is a more manageable writing task; (2) there are far more opportunities for publication; and (3) article-length publications lend themselves to expansion into book-length works later on.

A simple way to begin, a way that can help you settle on a topic and on a potential publisher, is to fill in the blanks in the exercise that follows.

EXERCISE

I could write a pretty decent article about _____(a)_____ which might be similar to the kinds of articles I read in _____(b)_____. Most of the articles in (b) are about _____ words in length and do/do not have references, charts, illustrations.

To be useful, your reponse in (a) should be reasonably specific. For example

> *Right:* "I could write a pretty decent article about how I used a class field trip to the Botanic Gardens to teach my sixth-graders an ecology lesson about plant environments."

> *Wrong:* "I could write a pretty decent article about how present educational systems fail to help further the condition of mankind."

While the right choice above lists a specific application, one that will certainly be of interest to many other teachers, the wrong choice is too global and imprecise to be of much use to anyone. If it could be made more specific, its philosophic goals would be more attainable.

Consider this example:

> *Right:* "I could write a pretty decent article about how I went about setting up a lucrative consulting business in my spare time, giving concrete examples of how I saved many large companies money and time by providing them with expertise they could not get in-house."

> *Wrong:* "I could write about the general value for companies of using outside consultants rather than depending entirely on in-house staff."

Here, too, the difference between the right approach and the wrong one are the lines between the specific and the general, the practical and the theoretical.

This is not to suggest that there is no place for theoretical articles or viewpoints that transcend the practical. Profound implications may ultimately emerge from your article, to be sure, but it is generally not a good idea to go into the project hoping to be profound. In fact, the more specific you are, the more down to earth, the better chance you have of getting your ideas on paper – and of ultimately seeing them in print.

There is no reason why your response in (b) has to be limited to a single magazine or professional journal. You may list several that seem appropriate for your proposed article. What is important, however, is that you select periodicals that reflect the type of article you are planning to write. If your proposed article is a practical discussion about supervising retail store employees, don't select a journal with a theoretical emphasis on marketing and retailing. If your article presents a technical, research-based study on hospital management, don't choose a periodical that concentrates on practical articles on how to run a hospital. Rather, try to find a magazine whose tone and content is as close to your proposed article as possible. The best way to find out the emphasis of a periodical in is to look through recent issues to get a sense of the kinds of materials and range of styles and topics the editors prefer.

Where to find lists of periodicals. If you are unable to think of magazines or journals off the top of your head, there are three main sources of information about periodicals in the library. The most comprehensive, *Ulrich's International Periodicals Directory,* which you can find in just about any library, small or large, lists all the journals and magazines appropriate to your field by subject matter. *Ulrich's* is international in scope, which is helpful to the prospective author since many foreign periodicals are eager for the advice and insights of successful professionals in the United States.

The *Standard Periodical Directory* overlaps with *Ulrich's* but includes more periodicals published in the United States and Canada. It lists over 66,000 periodicals, including general interest magazines, professional and trade journals, government and organization journals, directories, house organs, university and alumni publications, proceedings of scientific and academic societies, specialized business publications, literary, bibliographic, and library publications, and more.

MIMP (Magazine Industry Market Place) is a comprehensive guide and a central reference tool in the magazine publishing industry. *MIMP* lists virtually every major publication and categorizes each by the type of material emphasized and preferred. It provides the names, addresses, and phone numbers of editors and gives some information about the periodical, both of which are especially useful in making the initial contact.

After compiling a list of the names and addresses of the possible journals, you might want to send for a recent issue to get a sense of the types of articles they publish, the level of the articles, to whom they are addressed, and their length and format. Also, a recent issue of a journal might give you the manuscript requirements, including whether or not unsolicited articles will be read, as well as the editorial address to which material or a query letter should be sent.

Appendix B contains a list of about 70 journals, organized by subject area. This should help you identify those journals that have a liberal policy regarding unsolicited manuscripts from new authors and which would be most suitable for your topic.

Book-Length Works
Whether or not you have already published articles in the professional or trade periodicals, you may now be thinking about a book-length project. Perhaps some of the people who have read your articles are encouraging

you to write a longer work. Or perhaps you've read about college professors, economists, accountants, and other professionals who earn in excess of $100,000 from their highly successful textbooks. In any case, if now you are thinking of writing a book-length project, there are a few things that should be clarified at the beginning.

Most book-length projects can be developed in one of three ways: as a textbook, a scholarly/technical book, or a trade book. In the publishing field, an important distinction is made between a "trade" book and "text" book. The distinction is practical, not theoretical. It is so fundamentally accepted that in almost all publishing companies there are separate editors for trade and text books, and usually completely separate divisions. Some publishers, such as Bobbs-Merrill, Harcourt Brace Jovanovich, and Holt, Rinehart & Winston even have separate buildings, half a continent or more apart, for trade books and texts. It is imperative at the outset, therefore, that you know if you are developing a potential trade book or text book.

Trade books. A trade book is a book intended for purchase by the general public and by libraries. It is generally sold through bookstores and book clubs, directly to the reader.

It may be fiction or nonfiction, hardcover or paperback. Paperbacks have become a potent force in publishing during the past ten years, often generating significantly higher sales and royalties earnings than hardcover books. The prospective author should carefully evaluate the possibility of paperback publication, a possibility overlooked by many of us raised in the hardcover milieu of traditional publishing.

Paperback books are divided into two types: trade paperbacks and mass market paperbacks. Trade paperbacks are marketed in the same ways as hardcover trade books. They are sold in the same bookstores, at the same trade discount. They are relatively new on the scene, only ten to fifteen years old. A trade paperback may be an original title, a reprint of a classic or contemporary work, or may be issued simultaneously with the hardcover original. This last practice is becoming popular when the publisher feels the author has the audience to sell enough copies in short enough time to make it worthwhile. Recent novels by Kurt Vonnegut, for example, have been issued simultaneously in hardcover and trade paperback versions. The trade paperback – unlike the mass market paperback – tends to get reviewed and is generally accorded the same respect as a hardcover book.

Mass market paperbacks are the rack-sized reprints we think about when we hear the word paperback. They are sold not only in book stores, but in bus stations, at newsstands, and in drug stores as well. While about half the mass market paperbacks are now comprised of original titles not previously available in hardcover, this market is typically associated with reprints of books issued previously in hardcover. Most of the mass market originals are "genre" books, such as romances, mysteries, or science fiction.

A trade book may be a commercial blockbuster, such as a Harold Robbins bestseller, or it may be a fairly technical work of great intellectual merit, such as Stephen Jay Gould's *The Mismeasure of Man* or Morton Hunt's *The Universe Within*. A trade book may be designed to appeal to the broad population, or to some specified audience, such as the mystery or science fiction buff. A trade book may also appeal to a very specialized audience, such as a book on how to operate a ham radio, how to identify mushrooms in the country, or a book discussing the directors of every movie made by an American studio. In all these cases, they are trade books because they are selected and purchased by the people who will read them or by a library.

Many business and professional persons, experts, consultants, and teachers have parlayed their professional expertise into highly successful and very profitable trade books. The reading public is always eager to learn the workings of a profession from the inside, which explains the success of such books as veteran police officer Joseph Wambaugh's novels of police life, beginning with his first, *The New Centurions*, or former nun Mary Gilligan Wong's life inside the convent, *Nun*. Dr. David Viscott's *The Making of a Psychiatrist* and the mysterious Dr. X's *Intern* both became bestsellers by offering a no-holds-barred look at the medical profession from one who was inside. Offering the lay reader some professional insight that is useful in making important decisions accounts for the continued popularity of one of the most successful trade books of all time, Dr. Benjamin Spock's *Baby and Child Care*. A dramatic clinical case study, such as Dr. Theodore Isaac Rubin's *Lisa and David* or *Sybil* by Flora Rheta Schreiber is always a sure bet for success if it is well executed. The "how-to" and "self-help" genres, either psychological or practical have made a success of mail order industry consultant Maxwell Sroge's practical guide on how to get in on the mail order business, *Inside the Leading Mail Order Houses*. Psychological self-help books have a booming market, typified by counselor Wayne Dyer's pop-psych epic, *Your Erroneous Zones*, psychologist Herbert J. Freudenberger's, (with Geraldine Richardson) *Burn-Out*, sex researcher Alex Comfort's *Joy of Sex* and Stanley Nass's & Manfred Weidhorn's highly entertaining *Turn Your Life Around*.

Business expertise has been turned into a publishing phenomenon time and again with such books as consultant John Naisbitt's *Megatrends* or Kenneth Blanchard's and Spencer Johnson's *The One Minute Manager* or William E. Donoghue's *No-Load Mutual Fund Guide*.

These are but a few of the hundreds of examples of consultants, teachers, or experts in one field who turned their expertise into bestselling trade books.

Textbooks. A textbook, on the other hand, is designed to be used by students in an existing course of study. For a textbook to be published, there has to be a potential market of identifiable students for it – a course or program that requires it. No publisher would be interested in considering a textbook if there were no one to use it.

One major difference between trade and textbooks is that whereas a trade book is generally selected by the person who reads it, a textbook is generally selected by an instructor, an academic department or committee, or a school system through its school board or curriculum advisors. This decision may well affect hundreds or even thousands of students who will read the book, and often the success of a text depends on just a few large "adoptions" – decisions to use the book in an institution. An introduction to economics text adopted at Ohio State University may sell 3,000 copies – at just that one institution! This affects the way the book is sold and how the book is discounted to the bookseller, with trade books generally discounted 40% and texts discounted 20%. This means that a trade book which retails for $15.00 will be sold to the bookstore for $9.00, while a textbook that sells for $15.00 will cost the bookstore $12.00. The difference in markup reflects the fact that the bookstore is likely to order and sell dozens, hundreds, or even thousands of the textbook without any of its own marketing efforts, while trade book sales will be more sporadic and unpredictable, usually requiring some marketing effort by the book seller.

Of course, many times trade books are used in courses, especially as supplementary reading. B. F. Skinner's *Walden Two* and Margaret Mead's *Coming of Age in Somoa* still sell widely in college bookstores, decades after their original publication. Sometimes, when this becomes apparent to a publisher, such as in the case of a classic novel, the publisher will issue the same novel in a textbook edition, adding a scholarly preface and some footnotes – and often charging up to twice the price. Books such as *Crime and Punishment* or even such modern classics as Vladimir Nabokov's *Lolita* are available in inexpensive mass market paperback and more expensive school editions, with annotations, footnotes, and other scholarly paraphernalia.

The first question that has to be addressed as you formulate your book-length project is, "Is a textbook what I should be doing?" You may find as you explore this question that perhaps you should be thinking not of a textbook, but rather of a trade book, or even a scholarly/technical book – two alternatives many prospective textbook writers ultimately realize would be preferable for them.

Technical and scholarly books. A third category of book is the "technical" or "scholarly" book. Unlike the textbook, this is intended primarily for individual or library purchase; but unlike the trade book, its potential sales are very small and it audience very limited. Therefore, in order for it to be profitable for a publisher, it has to be sold at a considerably higher price and marketed in a specialized way. For example, Academic Press, which specializes in scholarly behavioral science books, offers Brandstatter & Davis's *Group Decision Making* for $45.00, a hefty price for a book of less than 600 pages without illustrations. But they are marketing the book to specialists in that field, to technical libraries, and to corporations that may find the information valuable. Nichols Publishing, another scholarly house with a large list in business and engineering, sells Odell & Rosing's 300 page, *The Future of Oil* for $47.50—a price that specialists in the field are willing to pay for this technically-oriented book by expert energy forecasters.

One way of marketing such books is through direct mail promotion, where a publisher can identify and reach a target audience (such as psychologists) by purchasing mailing lists from professional organizations and journals (such as the American Psychological Association). The *Encyclopedia of Associations,* which we discuss in chapter 4, is an excellent resource for obtaining specialized mailing lists for direct-mail marketing.

This trade/text/scholarly distinction—a distinction based on who ultimately selects a book and who purchases it—has implications that affect everything you do, from the development of the prospectus that you send the publisher, to the actual writing of your book, to the way it is marketed and sold. But mostly, it affects at the very beginning how you go about deciding whether you should be writing a textbook at all—or whether you should be thinking of some other type of book into which you channel your energies.

Making your decision. The first question you might ask yourself is, "If published, where would my book be used? Who would buy it?" Identifying clearly the potential reader or groups of readers, the educational level for which it is geared, and its likely audiences and markets is necessary at the outset. The more specific your answers, the better your chances of publication. Even if you have decided your work is a text book, you must still decide between high school level, elementary level, or college level, since textbooks for elementary and high school are handled quite differently from college and graduate school texts. In fact, just as the difference between trade and textbooks results in separate divisions at a publishing house, so too the difference between "el-hi" and "college" level texts results in separate divisions. I once wrote a text on introductory psychology that the reviewers felt could be used in both community college courses and high school courses. But because my publisher's el-hi division and college division had so little contact and were in such stiff competition with each other, it was decided not to market the book to high school courses, thus eliminating a large segment of the potential market.

Sometimes, a book will have more than one likely readership and hence, more than one potential market. A colleague of mine was working on a book for use in teaching reading skills in the primary grades. She was well along in her work when she found out from the publishers whom she solicited that all those who were willing to support such a project wanted to design their own book and hire their own writers. This is especially true in certain fields such as elementary and secondary education texts or with reference books. She became disheartened and was about to abandon the project when, through a recommendation, I got to look at it.

I pointed out to her that in addition to the market she originally had in mind, there was another market – quite a large one too – that she should consider. It is called the "academic skills" market, a euphemism for remediation, and it is typically handled by the pubisher's college division. Her book, I thought, would be ideal for college freshmen in need of intensive remedial skills. I knew there were many courses designed for just such a purpose. She submitted it to several publishers, through their college divisions, and found acceptance quite soon. Of course, she had to make a few changes in her examples and her tone, but this was relatively easy to do. Also, since she now knew exactly who would be reading the book it was much easier to write it.

The question of who would use your book demands not only that you identify the level of its intended readership, but if it is intended as a book you should also identify the specific course(s), or the part of the curriculum, for which it could be used. There is a major difference between writing a textbook for an introduction to data processing course and an advanced text on IBM 3070 assembly language. The difference is not only in the size of the potential audience (the former being much larger than the latter) and in the way the book would be marketed by the sales staff, but also in the credentials and background the author would be expected to have and the kind of experts required to review the book prior to publication. These are summarized in the table on pages 14-15.

You don't have to be well known in your field to write a textbook – but it does help. The term "well known" can mean many different things. It can mean that you have published prolifically in the professional journals or that you have been a frequent lecturer at meetings, conferences, and professional organizations. It can mean that your work is cited in other texts and articles and that your name has a high recognition factor to those who might be adopting your book. But, as I mentioned, it is not necessary to have a reputation in order to get a book

Table 1.1

TEXT, TRADE OR SCHOLARLY BOOK: A COMPARISON IN THE PSYCHOLOGY FIELD

Book Type	Title/ Author	Marketing	Suggested Price	Author Expertise	Expected Sales
Text	*Abnormal Psychology* (Harmatz)	College under-graduate courses	469 pp. $19.95	Not known for original work – college professor	20,000
Schol/ Tech.	*Neurosis and The Social Environment* (Byrne & Duncan-Jones)	Direct mail Conventions Journal advtg.	296 pp. $32.50	Known for having made original contributions in field	1,200
Trade	*Turn Your Life Around* (Nass & Weidhorn)	Bookstore display/ TV shows Mail Catalog Advertising in mass media	219 pp. $10.95	Neither had published in psychology before: Both college professors	1,500
Trade	*Buying Country Property* (Irving Price)	Widely advertised in newspapers and magazine/ Book Club selection	172 pp. $9.95	Twenty-five years of real estate experience	50,000

Trade	*Naturebirth: You, Your Body and Your Baby* (Dana Brook)	Hardcover and paperback printings, Marketed in bookstores, Advertised in magazines	270 pp. $6.95 paper	Midwife and mother of three	50,000
Schol./ Tech.	*The Guide to DP Training Courses: Descriptions of Over 300 Programs and Workshops* (ed. J.W. Franklin)	Direct mail to Corporate Trainers Advertised in technical journals	364 pp. $95.00	Edited by a person with much experience in the training field, including technical data processing training	1,500

published. My very first publication, in fact, was a college textbook – one that became a leader in its field – and no one had ever heard of me before. In my professional area, I became known through my textbook. In many fields, authors of leading texts were not widely known before their texts became leaders.

What is important – and what publishers will look for – is that you have had experience teaching the course for which you are writing the book and that you are familiar with the competing texts in the field, and their relative strengths and weaknesses. In some technical areas, however, publishers would be reluctant to sign up a project by an unknown, unless there is some compelling reason to do so. It is better in technical areas to have at least the beginnings of a reputation. A good track record of journal publications is generally the most persuasive entree into the area of technical/scholarly book publications, while professional achievement and recognition is a plus in trade publishing as well.

The trade book publisher will evaluate your professional expertise, as well as your ability to be persuasive in person and print. Many successful books, from Wayne Dyer's *Your Erroneous Zones* to John Naisbitt's *Megatrends* were launched to prominence by the radio and TV appearances of the author, each of whom has professional credibility in addition. The credentials are important for back flap copy: the persuasiveness and charisma for moving the book in the market place.

There is no area of professional competence and expertise that is not suitable for a good trade book. Master auto mechanics William Crouse and Donald Anglin have done extremely well with their six successive editions of *Automotive Manual Transmission and Power Trains*. Hardly a catchy title, but it sells. So too does a book by three physicians who specialize in – of all things – thyroid disease: Lawrence C. Wood, David S. Cooper and E. Chester Ridgway's, *Your Thyroid: A Home Reference*.

Experts and professionals in such non-esoteric fields as veterinary medicine (James Herriot's *All Things Bright and Beautiful*), law (Alan Dershowtiz's *The Best Defense*), and cosmetics (Jerome Alexander & Roberta Ellis, *Be Your Own Makeup Artist*) have all succeeded at writing successful trade books by combining their professional insights with a sense of candor, wit, and appropriateness.

Assessing Your Situation

Now that we have surveyed the general publishing situation, let us summarize the main ideas up to this point.

1. Virtually every professional person has something of value to say about his or her field of expertise. Narrowing down what it is you have to say begins the process of writing about it.

2. After deciding what you have to say, you have to decide how to

say it – and to whom. This entails defining the market (or audience) you wish to reach. At this point, you will decide between an article for a professional journal or for a popular magazine, a textbook, a technical/scholarly/professional book (including reference works), or a nontechnical trade book.

3. Several predictable reasons deter professional persons from pursuing a project they think viable. The most common reasons are not believing you have something important to say, failure to understand the market, or lack of confidence in your writing abilities. All of these, when viewed in the proper perspective, can be overcome.

With these principles, let us begin to focus on what you can do to begin developing your project. If you don't have an idea already, you may begin by asking yourself several questions.

1. What are some factors to which I attribute my professional successes?

2. What are some of the things I've noticed that need improvement in my field?

3. Is there an interesting case or situation I worked on or came across recently that others in my profession might learn from?

4. Would some of the "tricks" of my trade be of interest to the general public, as consumers or clients of my profession?

5. Can I apply some of the insights from my professional field to general kinds of problems directly outside my professional purview?

Here are a few examples that might be helpful in answering some of these questions. Dr. Sandy Richler, a young podiatrist, built up a large practice in a relatively short time. When he asked himself question 1, he came up with half a dozen solid reasons, from his advertising and initial patient contact to his accurate file keeping procedures for follow-ups (recalls, as they are called in the profession), to his general attitude toward patients. I advised him to make some notes about these factors, and the notes became the germ for an article – "Getting Started in Practice: Ten Rules of Thumb for Foot Doctors" – that appeared in a business-oriented podiatric magazine.

Paul and Mary Bland's Country Comfort Restaurant was doing just fine with the sophisticated city crowd who journeyed two-and-a-half hours into the hills for what they knew would be a consummate dinner. I had dined there several times and was impressed not only with the food but with my hosts' charm and ebullience as well. They were also extremely generous in giving out the recipes for some of their most special appetizers and entrees. I suggested one evening, over a postprandial Pernod, that they put some of their recipes in an article for a gourmet magazine. "But we can't write," Mary protested. "And we don't have much time for writing," Paul added, "with our running the inn and all." I understood, but insisted that if they could take only a few minutes each morning to get the recipes down they would probably become enthused enough to write the narrative that gives recipe articles their charm. "And," I pointed out, "you have lots of photographers as friends. Why don't you have some pictures taken of the inn and some of your colorful dishes, along with some shots of the customers contentedly dining, and send the pictures in with the article."

Answering question 2, Todd Beuhler, an antique dealer who had expressed an interest in writing but didn't know what to write about, laughed aloud and said, "I could write ten volumes on things I've noticed that need improvement in my field. You wouldn't believe it."

"Okay," I said, "name a few."

"Well, to begin with, here the rule *caveat emptor* is often abused beyond excuse. I mean people are really taken advantage of. Also, most people not only don't have any idea what they are buying, but don't even know the right questions to ask. Then, there's the whole issue of insurance. You see, when you buy. . . ."

He went on for a good half hour. When he stopped, I asked, "Why don't you write up these ideas for an article or book? I'm sure a lot of prospective antique buyers would be interested."

"Ahh," he shrugged, "there's a million things written about this." His excuse was one of the most common – the belief that "I have nothing new to say."

"But," said I, "if a million things have already been written and these abuses are still happening, then nothing has been effective yet. Maybe it's time for something new to supplement those million things: something that can help people who don't even know about the other things." We went on to explore the kinds of magazines that amateur antique collectors are likely to read, and I suggested he go over some of the articles in recent issues to get a feeling for what they were looking for. And so began his article which was eventually published in a popular magazine.

Julie Conners, an attorney, found the source for her article in answering question 3. "This didn't happen to me," she explained, "but to one of my colleagues. It's a fear many attorneys have, and a tricky legal situation when it does occur, so I think it may interest a lot of lawyers." This is her scenario: A man had a new will drawn up by his attorney. Because of delays in the attorney's hectic office, several weeks go by and the document still isn't typed up. The man sends a short note asking that it please be expedited since he is leaving soon on a trip. It is then typed and mailed, along with a letter from the attorney raising a few questions and suggesting some changes. But before the will and letter reach the man, he drops dead of a sudden heart attack. All his potential heirs – including two ex-wives, a widow, a parent, a nephew, and three children, one of whom was adopted – are drawn into the complex probate battle, and the man's dilatory attorney is being threatened with several malpractice suits.

The situation was dramatic, full of human interest value. It also had many interesting legal implications backed by hundreds of precedents, Julie explained, that varied from jurisdiction to jurisdiction. Julie knew of several magazines that ran practical articles for lawyers. We also considered the possibility of writing it up as a human interest story for a nonlegal magazine, but her inclinations in writing and her approach to the subject matter reduced that option. As Julie began drafting the story, she more and more focused on the journal to which she thought it should be sent. As it developed, its tone and audience became more clear and it was finally published in one of the lively journals for young, iconoclastic attorneys.

Question 4 implies that you should look for your writing ideas in what you do every day. It may not seem revelational to you, but the sum of your daily professional activities is often ideal as the germ of a good article. The optician can write an exciting article about how to look your best in glasses, and the computer consultant can write a catchy article about how to buy a business computer. Think about who would want to read it, what magazine would publish it – and you are on your way to defining your audience. In this way you can use your technical knowledge to create a popular article. Jenns Husted and Chris Ryman, technical directors of a ski school, turned their technical knowledge on how to negotiate a short-radius turn into a nontechnical article for the popular magazine, *Skiing*. You can also apply your knowledge outside your field. Professional gambler Robert Dietz applied his handicapping knowledge to scientific methodology for an interesting article on "Scientists, Gamblers & Magicians," which he published in a popular science magazine.

In answering question 4 – about the tricks of the trade – Wynne, an ex-convict now in college trying to straighten himself out, found his story idea. "When I was junkie," he told me, "I must have pulled over a thousand burglaries, most of them in the daytime. I hit every neighborhood in this city."

As I discussed it with Wynne, I found out that on each block he would pick out one or two houses to hit. It was the homeowners themselves who guided him right to their house. "If you're going out about three in the afternoon and expect to return late at night," he asked me, "do you put on your outside lights?" I thought about it and answered honestly. "Yes, I do leave them on when I know I'll be returning home after dark."

"Then you're a cooperative victim," he rejoined. "You see, what I would do is drive around an area like yours a couple of hours before dusk, let's say about three or four on a Saturday afternoon. When I'd see a house with the outside lights on, while it was still light out, I could safely assume the people were gone and wouldn't be home till after dark. It gave me plenty of time to explore the place at my leisure."

This and other tricks of the trade became the basis of his article on expert advice from a burglar, written for a general magazine audience.

Question 5 has provided many an author with the basis for an excellent article or book. Most of us at times have discovered methods of proven success in the course of our professional activities that can be applied elsewhere—in other professions. Take the case of Rodney O'Rourke, a sales representative for a large paper products company. He found that he was gradually becoming overwhelmed by all the paper work and record keeping his job entailed. Both of these functions were necessary to keep current on accounts and sales, but they were taking an unreasonable amount of time, detracting from his other functions. People in most fields can identify with this situation.

He decided to buy a microcomputer with an appropriate data management package. This allowed him to set up his own customized records without having to learn any programming. In a short time, he found this new system significantly eased his file-keeping burden, and allowed him more time to concentrate on customer sales and personal contacts. Realizing that many other sales representatives could empathize with this type of situation, he wrote an article detailing how the system works and how it helped his business. One of the themes of the article is that you don't have to be a computer expert to benefit from a computer in your business. He chose to publish it in a popular (as opposed to technical) computer magazine, *Creative Computing,* where it would reach an audience interested in using microcomputers in a variety of professions and fields, in addition to sales. In this way, business people who were not in sales but had the same paperwork problems, could have access to his experiences.

Now that you have seen how to assess your situation and have begun to focus on what you are going to do, let's look in more detail at how to develop your project; that is, how to move from the thinking stages into real planning and development.

2

Developing Your Project

One thing that differentiates the real writer from the amateur – or even the successfully published amateur writer from the frustrated, bitter, unpublished one – is the way the real writer decides on what to write, how to approach a particular subject, and how to develop the topic following the initial decision. The real writer never views a writing project simply in its "inspirational" phase – as the burst of a great idea that he or she is sure everyone will enjoy reading – but rather perseveres in finding a practical way to reach an audience, who will eventually read and react to what the writer wants to say. Before writing, a real writer honestly assesses his or her ability to undertake the project, dispassionately consider the project's publication possibilities, and logically defines the audience he or she hopes to reach.

The process of how a successful writer develops a project has four distinct stages.

1. *Inspiration:* A fabulous idea comes to mind, usually in the middle of daydreaming about something else, before going to sleep at night, waiting on line at the bank, sitting in the courtroom, driving to work, or at some other unlikely place or time. You play with idea for awhile and become convinced it is great. You begin to fantasize about your colleagues' new respect after reading your article . . . or envision your appearance on a national TV talk show with your new book. You've always wanted to see your name in print, and now the inspiration is here.

2. *Preparation:* It was Thomas Edison who said, "Genius is one percent inspiration and ninety-nine percent perspiration." If stage one is one percent of the work, then the preparational stage begins the next ninety-nine percent. After cooling off for a few days, during which time the sen-

sible person disregards about ninety-five percent of the bold ideas conceived in the ecstasy of inspiration, you should begin to assess the project more realistically. Can I give what such a project demands, in terms of my time, research abilities, and writing strengths? Would enough people really be interested in reading about what I have to say? Am I going to put in the energy to carry it through to completion, or will it become one more unfinished plan in my life? If you answer these questions to your satisfaction, you can begin to define the scope of your project and identify the market you want to reach. Then, through the development of your prospectus or preliminary outline, you will begin to make headway in the writing itself.

3. *Writing:* The stage that separates the doers from the self-deceivers. This is the true test of whether you have it in you, whether you can bear the loneliness and almost inhuman perseverance and self-criticism it takes to be a writer. This is the stage where your ability to organize your time productively with single-minded determination will be challenged by every imaginable distraction, and then some. At this stage you will be tested in your ability to listen openly to and accept others' criticisms about your work – an intimate part of your ego when you are in the midst of writing – and to generate your own self-criticism. This is the stage where the transition from ideas in your head to words on paper is given its acid test.

4. *Publication:* Of course, this is the most exciting part. Your work is finally in the process of being published. But you will find there are still a thousand and one things to do, last minute chores that demand attention. This stage, which begins when the final manuscript has been accepted for publication, includes all the production demands, picky little problems and detail work with which published writers are familiar: putting together an art program, keeping a permissions file, reading and correcting galleys and page proofs, and indexing the book-length project. These small details can add to the success and quick publication of certain types of projects.

In this chapter we focus on preparation, particularly on how the prospective writer defines the market (audience) and begins to approach the project from a practical standpoint. In the following chapters we will then focus in detail on stages 3 and 4.

Defining the Market

The successful writer always writes with a specific market in mind. The market may be (1) a group with some particular expertise (periodontists), (2) people with certain kinds of problems (insomniacs, people on the verge of personal bankruptcy, sexually frustrated individuals), (3) people with particular interests (travelers to India on a limited budget, vegetarians who cook Szechuan Chinese dishes), (4) people with a special need to know some technical information (owners of microcomputers, a person considering a career in law enforcement, a person planning to buy country property), (5) students in elementary school, high school, college, or graduate courses, or (6) a segment of the general public. Any writer who feels he is writing for everyone is probably writing for no one but himself. The table on pages 24-25 shows how various professionals may choose to reach any of the specific audiences mentioned here, and how this choice affects what they write about and influences how they conceptualize their projects.

A few key rules of defining your potential audience and shaping your writing project emerge from this table. Let's review some of these rules as we look over the table. Begin to consider in your own mind which rules apply to you. You can fill in the Pre-Prospectus Exercise (page 36) as you go along, to get a better grip on how to go about developing your proposal.

First, notice how our attorney, who primarily practices landlord/ tenant law, can approach her writing project from three possible vantage points. For one, she can write for the general public, including all kinds of information about the law, in an article or book called *Know Your Legal Rights.* She might submit this to a general interest magazine, such as *Parade*, or since so few general interest magazines are left, she might slant the article to women's interests and develop it for a magazine such as *Redbook* or *Ladies' Home Journal.* In either case, she would have to be sure to include enough information about enough topics, along with sufficient examples and illustrations, to attract and hold the interest of a large audience. Her expertise in all these topics might not be a concern if the article or book is designed for the general public. If she were writing about contracts for specialists, or even a book about wills and probate for the general public, she would be expected to be a specialist in those areas. But for a wide-ranging book for the entire public, her qualifications as a practicing lawyer are probably sufficient.

A book-length project such as *Know Your Legal Rights* would only interest a publisher if the author can show what makes it special – how it distinguishes itself from similar titles and how it can be marketed, since there are so many similar books available. When the author is able to demonstrate its sales potential, the publisher can then make a probable assessment of the market. Upon publication then, the publisher would see to it that all these selling points are featured on the jacket and in the advertising.

A second possibility for our attorney is that she can write about her professional specialization – landlord and tenant law. She knows this area extremely well, has a large resource of case material from which to

Table 2.1

DEFINING THE APPROPRIATE AUDIENCE

Audience	Writer	Title and Topic
General public	Lawyer	*Know Your Legal Rights* – – General information about all areas of law, such as contracts, traffic, business, criminal.
Apartment dwellers	Lawyer	*Up Your Landlord* – Tenant rights information.
Attorneys	Lawyer	*Effective Strategies for Cross-Examination* – How to cross-examine witnesses during litigation.
General public	Denist	*Flossing: It Could Save Your Teeth* – How a regimented flossing program can prevent periodontal disease responsible for most tooth loss in middle age.
Dental surgeons	Dentist	*Submaxillary Prosthesis for Patients Undergoing Rhino-mastoplastic Surgery* – Technical procedure with illustrations.
All women	Dermatologist	*Beauty and Skin Care* – Hints on how to keep skin smooth and healthy.
Older women	Dermatologist	*Golden Skin for the Golden Years* – Same as above, except with examples and information geared to the older women.

Men and women	*Skin Successes* – Much the same as above, except with special sections on men's skin problems (shaving, jock itch, etc.) and more examples for both men and women.
Lay (amateur) investors	*Leveraging Your Future in a Bear Market* – How to manipulate your stocks for ultimate gain, written for *Money* magazine.
Professional investors	*Using UCSD-based Fortran Programs to Compute Rho Variables in Economic Forecasting* – A technical article for professional journals.
Owners of home computers	*Getting the Most Out of Your Computer's Graphics* – How to do graphic programs for Atari, Commodore, and other home computers, written for magazine such as *Popular Computing*.
Professional software developers	*Budgeting Your OEM's Time in Development of Forth-based Utilities* – A highly technical article for an electronic engineering and professional computing journal.

Note: "Dermatologist" appears aligned with "Men and women", "Investment counselor" with "Lay (amateur) investors", "Investment counselor" with "Professional investors", "Programmers" with "Owners of home computers", and "Programmer" with "Professional software developers".

draw, and it is of interest to millions of people. Magazines such as *Apartment Life* have a young readership made up primarily of tenants who would want to read an article on the subject.

The book market would be relatively small, although potential purchasers would probably pay more for the book if it solved some important problems for them. Also, the marketing of the book would be reasonably well-defined by its subject matter: the publisher would know, for example, that it is a waste of time to market it in areas where there are only single-family homes, and therefore no tenant/landlord problems. There is mail order potential here, too, since the book could be marketed through magazines such as *Apartment Life* that cater to apartment dwelling tenants.

Finally, there is another route through which she can approach publication. She may want to develop an article from her senior thesis at law school, a thesis incidentally that won second prize in a competition. This would not make her much money, to be sure, but it is impressive to show clients and colleagues that your ideas were published in a professional journal. Also, other attorneys may come across her name in the journal and that can be a potential source of referral.

So we see that our attorney has three possibilities for publishing.

1. The general public, slightly narrowed down.
2. A specialized segment of the public.
3. Other professionals in the same field.

Notice that in making this decision, the scope of the book or article (including its title) and the possible journals for which it is intended all become delineated.

Sometimes the decision is more clear-cut. When Dr. Condit wanted to publish the findings from three of his major cases in his specialized area of maxilo-facial reconstruction and prosthesis, there was no choice about where to publish or how to develop the article: it would be appropriate only for a professional journal and would interest only an audience of equally specialized professionals.

But our dermatologist, Dr. Onkawa, had a choice similar to the attorney's. We see in his choice how a general subject can be tailored to a variety of specialized audiences: to all women, to middle-aged women, or both men and women. The examples and some of the content would be dictated by this decision, while the dermatological facts, of course, would remain constant. The same is also true with the investment counselor and the programmer, both of whom have to decide at the outset the audience they wish to address.

This narrowing down, focusing in process is quite important for a practical reason. Since most periodicals and book publishers today are rather specialized, the writer cannot expect to appeal to everyone. This helps the writer decide where to send the material. Also, by narrowing the prospective audience for a project, you make it easier to outline your article or book, since some subject matter would automatically be restricted or necessarily included by the nature of the audience chosen.

Once you have narrowed down your subject, you are then ready to begin your work. If your project is book-length, it is imperative to prepare a trade book proposal or text book prospectus first. (Notice that the term prospectus is generally preferred in text publishing, while proposal is always used in trade books). In the following section we discuss the parts of the trade proposal and text prospectus, referring to the sample proposal on pages 28 to 31 and the sample prospectus on pages 32 to 36 by numbered sections along the way.

It is also important to decide at this point whether you have the material for a book or an article; and if you decide an article, to choose among an article in a professional journal, a popular magazine, or a specialized magazine. Many books have begun as articles in journals, and it is often easier to get moving if you know that you only have an article to write instead of a whole book.

Starting Your Proposal or Prospectus

Developing a proposal or prospectus for a book is one way both to clarify in one's own mind the possible markets and to make the idea of a book-length project appealing to a publisher. Most editors are impressed by the prospective author who knows the market. As you develop your trade book proposal or text book prospectus you will find it forces you to think through many of the key questions about your project, even to the extent of having to decide if it is the right project for you or not. In the following sections, I show a step-by-step procedure to develop the proposal and prospectus.

A sample proposal and prospectus are shown here: one for a trade book – *How to Start and Run Your Own Word Processing Business* – that will soon be published by the same publisher who brought out the book you are now reading (Pages 28 to 31) and one for a college level textbook on life-span human development (Pages 32 to 36), a popular course in psychology departments. Both of these samples are typical of effective prospectuses of their type.

We should note at the outset that there are both obvious and more subtle differences between a trade book proposal and a textbook proposal. Generally, the decision to pursue either trade or text should be made prior to the development of a proposal or prospectus. But, if that decision has not yet been made, it is altogether possible that the development of the proposal or prospectus will help you make that decision.

A Proposal For

HOW TO START AND RUN YOUR OWN WORD PROCESSING BUSINESS   ◄── **1**

Gary S. Belkin

How to Run Your Own Word Processing Business is designed◄── **2**
for:

* the owner of a word processor or personal microcomputer
  (TRS, Apple, IBM, Commodore, Osborne, etc.), who is
  considering running a part-time or full-time word
  processing business at home.

* the secretary, administrative assistant, typist, or
  temporary office worker, looking to make an independent
  career with a word processing business.

* the student of typing, word processing or secretarial
  studies at the high school, business school, and
  community college level (where such courses are typically offered), who wants to parlay his or her newly
  acquired skills into a profitable, low-risk, after-school
  business.

* the business professional--attorney, small business
  owner, administrator, accountant, manager, executive,
  or academic--who wants to use the business's word
  processor to generate extra income or to pay for
  itself.

The book offers detailed information about how to start
your own word processing business with a minimum of capital
investment and how to run it on a day-to-day basis, effi-
ciently and economically, while fully exploiting its potential. You learn to use your personal, technical, and
business skills and contacts to attract clients and to
help finance the equipment you need.
It begins by introducing and surveying the entire field
of word processing, progressing from simple definitions of
what a word processing system is up to the latest applications of electronic data base system retrieval. The book
assumes no previous knowledge by the reader of computers or
information processing.

-1-

-2-

The author runs his own successful word processing business from home and over the past ten years has served as a business and technical consultant in the development of several successful business ventures, including a well-known word processing training school and a popular chain of typing (WP) and copy shops. He offers practical guidance about all aspects of running the business, from where to advertise up to what kind of equipment to buy (or rent or lease). These are just a few of the types of businesses the reader can begin to think about with a small personal computer or word processor.

- Typing service
- Word processing service bureau
- Operator training program
- Temporary and permanent WP operator placement agency
- Copy and typing service
- Indexing and copy editing services

The proposed book has several purchaser advantages and ◄————**3** strong marketing points. It can be marketed as part of the Wiley SMALL BUSINESS SERIES or it can be sold through direct mail channels. Since anyone who can type can easily learn to do word processing, the millions of individuals who are currently purchasing home and small business computers will want to consider the numerous possibilities for earning extra income from their investment. The tens of thousands of people who type at home for a living will be especially interested in turning a relatively small capital investment into a handsome profit for the equivalent hours of at-home labor.

Two points to emphasize:

First, it offers many <u>specific, practical examples</u> of ◄————**4** how to build up a word processing business that can be profitable with reference to different fields: Law; Accounting; Education; Advertising; Publishing; Resume Preparation; Insurance; Real Estate; Securities, Finance and Investment Banking; Marketing and Management. This will be an important selling feature, especially to the extent that it can be marketed to target buyers who will find these <u>specific-field applications and examples</u> relevant and useful for their potential business endeavors.

-3-

Second, its coverage of trade name hardware and software is broad enough to include virtually all the important
systems and programs available today, with detailed information about many of them. This brand-by-brand comparison
could be highlighted in the table of contents or index,
since many potential book purchasers are familiar with or
are considering several of these and would want to know more
about them. Included are discussions of such popular
systems or programs as:

APPLE-WRITER	AM JACQUARD	5
BENCHMARK	APPLE IIe/ LISA	
EASY WRITER	CPT	
GRAMMATIK	DEC RAINBOW	
MAGIC WINDOW	IBM MEMORY TYPEWRITERS	
PALANTIR	IBM DISPLAYWRITER	
PERFECT WRITER	IBM PC	
PERFECT SPELLER	KAYPRO	
PIE WRITER	LANIER NO PROBLEMS	
SCRIPSIT	LEXITRON	
SELECT	MICOM	
SPELLBINDER	NBI	
TI WRITER	WANG 25, OIS 130	
WORDSTAR	XEROX 820, 850 and 860	

-4-

Brief Table of Contents ◄─────────────── **6**

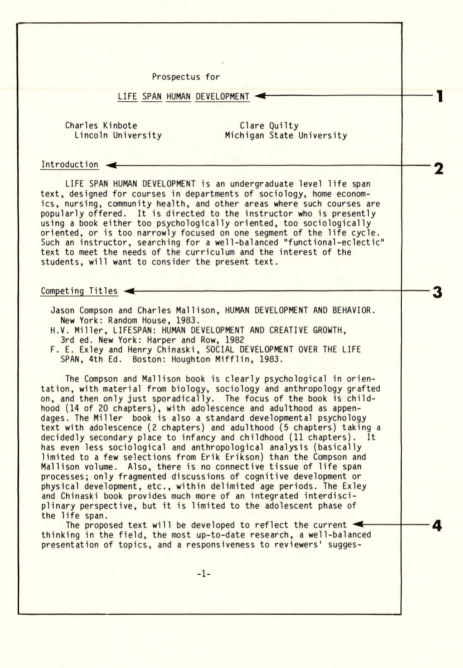

Prospectus for

<u>LIFE</u> <u>SPAN</u> <u>HUMAN</u> <u>DEVELOPMENT</u> ◄——————— **1**

Charles Kinbote   Clare Quilty
Lincoln University   Michigan State University

<u>Introduction</u> ◄——————————————— **2**

    LIFE SPAN HUMAN DEVELOPMENT is an undergraduate level life span
text, designed for courses in departments of sociology, home economics, nursing, community health, and other areas where such courses are
popularly offered. It is directed to the instructor who is presently
using a book either too psychologically oriented, too sociologically
oriented, or is too narrowly focused on one segment of the life cycle.
Such an instructor, searching for a well-balanced "functional-eclectic"
text to meet the needs of the curriculum and the interest of the
students, will want to consider the present text.

<u>Competing Titles</u> ◄——————————————— **3**

  Jason Compson and Charles Mallison, HUMAN DEVELOPMENT AND BEHAVIOR.
    New York: Random House, 1983.
  H.V. Miller, LIFESPAN: HUMAN DEVELOPMENT AND CREATIVE GROWTH,
    3rd ed. New York: Harper and Row, 1982
  F. E. Exley and Henry Chinaski, SOCIAL DEVELOPMENT OVER THE LIFE
    SPAN, 4th Ed. Boston: Houghton Mifflin, 1983.

    The Compson and Mallison book is clearly psychological in orien-
tation, with material from biology, sociology and anthropology grafted
on, and then only just sporadically. The focus of the book is childhood (14 of 20 chapters), with adolescence and adulthood as appen-
dages. The Miller book is also a standard developmental psychology
text with adolescence (2 chapters) and adulthood (5 chapters) taking a
decidedly secondary place to infancy and childhood (11 chapters). It
has even less sociological and anthropological analysis (basically
limited to a few selections from Erik Erikson) than the Compson and
Mallison volume. Also, there is no connective tissue of life span
processes; only fragmented discussions of cognitive development or
physical development, etc., within delimited age periods. The Exley
and Chinaski book provides much more of an integrated interdisci-
plinary perspective, but it is limited to the adolescent phase of
the life span.
    The proposed text will be developed to reflect the current ◄——— **4**
thinking in the field, the most up-to-date research, a well-balanced
presentation of topics, and a responsiveness to reviewers' sugges-

-1-

-2-

tions--all of which increase its adoption potential. The book is
designed at every step of the way with the needs of potential adopters
in mind. It is clearly written and rich in examples, and a program of
teaching and learning aids are developed simultaneously. Moreover,
it not only covers the requisite topics for its intended market, but
it is especially sensitive to the need for an eclectic point of view.
All too often in lifespan development texts, there is a lack of
functional integration between the physical, cultural, social, and
psychological dimensions of development throughout life. This results
both in a lack of relevance for the typical college reader and a
feeling of incompleteness or dissatisfaction on the part of the
instructor--who is relying more and more on paperbacks to attain the
perspective he or she wants.
        The proposed text will synthesize research findings and theoreti-
cal frameworks to show at each age level and stage of development how
individuals are shaped by and interact with a variety of historical,
social, and economic forces--some of which are beyond their control
to change--to develop in ways that reflect a synthesis of nature,
family nurture, and the more global impact of the cultural and social
milieu. The continuing impact of socialization over the course of
life will serve as an organizing principle throughout the book.
        The book also has several pedagogical features that should prove
to be strong selling points.

Pedagogical Aids

        To make the book interesting to students, a number of pedagogical
aids have been employed. For clarity and organization, the following
have been selected:
        •   Chapter Outlines (with brief capsulized summaries)
             open each chapter
        •   Annotated bibliographies at the conclusion of each
             chapter
        •   An art program designed for educational as well as
             aesthetic goals
        •   Marginal notes to highlight important terms and major
             concepts
        •   A glossary of relevant terms, including terms high-
             lighted in the book

        For high interest value, the book uses a research-based but
highly readable presentation. Many examples, with which students can
readily identify, are used for clarification. These examples help
make theoretical concepts especially relevant to the students' interests.

Special Topics Covered ◄─────────────────────── **5**

        In addition to the traditional topics, covered in all the books,
special attention is also directed toward important contemporary

-3-

issues in lifespan development. These selected topics have been shown by our informal "market research" (through discussions with our colleagues and examination of some typical lifespan syllabi) to be considered particularly relevant, important, and highly motivating to students. Many instructors are especially interested in one or several of these, and that could swing their adoption decision. These topics include:

- Career choices, implications, work adjustment, multiple/second careers--including women in the work force and dual-working couples

- Social class, values, and behavior

- Sociobiology or biosociology

- Gender-role learning, from infancy through senescence

- Impact of residential mobility and travel on family structure and on developing and maintaining important relationships

- The effect of family economic problems, such as unemployment, on aspects of development

- Sexuality, on-going relationships, and the climate of peer pressure

- The influence of television, music, and the mass media of com-munication on aspects of development

- Economic, health, social, and psychological components of aging

- The link between adolescents and senior citizens: marking time

-4-

<u>Brief Table of Contents</u> ◄───────────── **6**

LIFE SPAN HUMAN DEVELOPMENT

by Charles Kinbote and Clare Quilty

Introduction to the study of the Life Span

PART ONE: BASIC VIEWS

1. To Be Human: Nature and Nurture
2. Theories and Methods of Life Span Study

PART TWO: LIFE SPAN PROCESSES

3. Physical Development
4. Cognitive and Language Development
5. Attachment and Emotional Development
6. Moral Development
7. The Development of Identity

PART THREE: SOCIAL CONTEXTS OF DEVELOPMENT

8. The Intimate Environment of the Family
9. Equality and Hierarchy: Peers and School
10. Impersonal Contexts: The Mass Media
11. The Productive Matrix: Work

PART FOUR: THE HUMAN AGES: STAGES OF GROWTH AND DEVELOPMENT

12. Infancy and Childhood: The Beginnings
13. Youth: The Ambiguous and Transitional Stage
14. Maturity: The Search for a Place in the Sun
15. Aging: The Final Challenge

PART FIVE: EPILOGUE

16. Continuity and Change in Human Development

OUTLOOK: NEW DIRECTIONS IN LIFE SPAN DEVELOPMENT

PRE-PROSPECTUS EXERCISE

The general subject of which I wish to write is − − (a) − −. The kind of information I can best offer a reader, especially information that is somewhat different than what they can get elsewhere, is − − (b) − −. Based on my personal time and resources, the kind of project I should probably attempt is − − (c) − −.

-5-

Detailed Outline ◄────────────────── **7**

[Introduction to the study of the life span]

The reasons for studying human development are presented, and some of the basic methods of research are outlined. The rationale for an eclectic approach to the study of life span development is given.

===
PART ONE: BASIC VIEWS
===

This section provides a general overview of life span development ◄── **8**
and outlines the major theories and methods used in the study of human development. Chapter 1 discusses in some detail how heredity and environment intermix to influence the course of development. Chapter 2 outlines some of the theories used to explain the environmental role of development as well as some of the methods used to test out the theories and to gain new insights.

1. To Be Human: Nature and Nurture

The interaction between heredity and environment is discussed. A genetic primer outlines the role of genes, chromosomes, DNA, etc., and we evaluate the relative influence of heredity and environment on different aspects of development. The possibilities of genetic counseling (karyotyping) and the social implications of selection and assortive mating are considered.

2. Theories and Methods of Life Span Study

This chapter provides an integrated overview of the theoretical perspectives that help account for the physical, emotional, social, and cognitive dimensions of human development. After outlining the requirements for theory construction, the major theories of human development are introduced. Attention is also directed toward the ways we use different methodologies to investigate subtle aspects of an individual's total development over the course of life. The relationship between theory and research is considered.

===
PART TWO: INFANCY AND LIFE SPAN PROCESSES
===

3. Physical Development

Basic patterns of physical development from infancy through senescence are considered, along with major health problems and ial challenges that these bring about.

Parts of the Proposal or Prospectus

Although there are important differences between a trade book proposal, a textbook prospectus, and a scholarly book prospectus (which is usually no more than a letter and a reprint of articles on the proposed subject), there are certain basic principles that apply to them all. On the sample proposal and prospectus (pages 28-36), the bold numbers in the margins refer to the parts we discuss in this chapter. Let us look section by section at the basic parts of a typical prospectus or proposal, outlining some guidelines that may be helpful.

(1) Project Title, Author Name, Affiliation. Even at this very first juncture, where you would think everything is simple and direct, there are important decisions to make. What do you call your book? How do you identify yourself on the title page of the prospectus? Do you list your professional title and corporate or academic affiliation? Do you indicate your degree or professional licensure? Consider these possbilities.

<table>
<tr>
<td>Hearts of Conflict, Days of Storm
by Mimi Carter</td>
<td>Overcoming Grief and Mourning
by Mimi Carter, Ph.D.</td>
</tr>
</table>

— or —

<table>
<tr>
<td>This All Too Solid Flesh
by Dr. Bob Mason</td>
<td>A New Approach to Dieting
by Robert Mason, M.D.
Downstate Medical Center</td>
</tr>
</table>

The 30-Day Medical Diet
by Robert Mason, M.D.
Associate Professor, Downstate Medical Center
Director, LaMotta Diet Control Institute
South Orange, New Jersey

Very often writers, especially new writers, become infatuated with the title of their proposed work. In time the working title takes on a meaning to them that others cannot know about or that might mislead others. When psychotherapist Mimi Carter thought of her book, the proposed title, *Hearts of Conflict, Days of Storm*, invariably connoted to her all her theories on grief work and on ways of constructively dealing with death. But an editor looking over the title page of the prospectus would probably think, "Another bored housewife trying to write a romance." The second title, *Overcoming Grief and Mourning*, although not nearly as poetic, immediately alerts an editor who receives it what the work is about, and suggests by its tone and seriousness that the writer probably has some professional or academic credentials. Also, an editor who isn't interested himself may know of another editor in the same publishing house who is looking for a book on grief and mourning, and this direct title would alert him or her without further reading what the work is about.

A working title is fine for working, but don't hold on to it just out of habit. A poet, a Nobel Prize winner, at first called one of his master-pieces, "He Do the Police in Different Voices," and was reluctant to change the title when his friend and critic, Ezra Pound, suggested it. The title referred to a section of Charles Dickens's *Our Mutual Friend,* and the poet knew what it alluded to. But it didn't convey the meaning of the poem to the reader, and in the long run would probably detract from its seriousness. So finally T.S. Eliot changed the poem's title to the one we know today, "The Waste Land."

The choice of title is especially important in textbooks. In many textbooks areas certain commonly used titles—typically incorporating buzz words—immediately tell the potential adopter for which course the book is designed. The titles at the right are clearly meant for the courses at the left.

Introduction to Psychology	*Understanding People*
World History	*Civilization in Progress*
Counseling/Psychotherapy	*The Helping Relationship*

However, even in these cases it is better to use as a working title the most specific reference to what the book is about. If this bothers your aesthetic sensibilities too much, you can always put a tentative title underneath, as in:

Psychology: An Introduction
(tentative title: *Understanding People*)

Introduction to Word Processing
(working title)

Marketing: An Introduction
(A Multi-Perspective Approach)

Your name is not nearly as hard a decision as your book title, of course, but there are still a couple of things to think about. First, should you list your professional title or degree? The practice has changed with the times. Forty years ago, just about any book written by a person with a doctorate in philosophy, medicine, education, or law would list that im-mediately after the title, sometimes before, and at times both.

R.E. Ten Broek, Ph.D.
Dr. R.E. Ten Broek
Dr. R.E. Ten Broek, Ph.D.
—or even—
Stanley Chester, M.A., Oxford
Ph.D., Cambridge
LL.D. Yale

Writers and editors still don't fully agree on how this information should be communicated, in the book as well as in the prospectus, but the approach I suggest is to put all relevant information in your resume (vita). This will be discussed in chapter 4. Even with that information on your resume, what should go under the name on your prospectus? In many cases, little is necessary, but in some cases certain information helps.

If you have an academic affiliation, list it under your name for textbooks, scholarly, or technical books, but not necessarily for trade books. (Trade editors are often biased against academics, and think that a Ph.D.'s book won't be suitable for a trade audience.)

Introduction to Accounting
Felix Castelli
Baruch College, CUNY

Money Management for Young Couples
Felix Castelli, C.P.A.

Prepare Your Own Taxes
Felix Castelli
Baruch College, CUNY

If you have a corporate title and affiliation, list it if it is at all relevant to your project, but *omit* it if it might give a wrong idea of your interest in or ability to carry out the project.

Acceptable
The Assassination Conspiracy
Jane Leaky
The Detroit News-Herald

Climbing Up The Corporate Ladder
Howard Kammer, V.P.
Ford Motor Company

Unacceptable
The I-Love-Ice-Cream Diet
Franklin Wills, Chief
Ledgewood Police Dept.
Ledgewood Falls, NJ

Making It Big on Broadway
John Ramone, D.D.S.
Dentist, Private Practice

You can see in the samples that I did not list my university affiliation on the front page of the proposal for *How to Start and Run Your Own Word Processing Business*, since my academic affiliation would be irrelevant to my expertise in that business area. The authors of *Life Span Human Development*, on the other hand, did list their university affiliations, since this is important and relevant in a textbook prospectus. The query letter or resume enclosed with both, however, would identify fully the titles and affiliations of the authors.

(2) Introduction. In this short section, which should appear (or at least should begin) on the front page of the proposal or prospectus, the editor or reader will make the decision whether or not to read on. It should directly and concisely do four things.

- tell to whom the books is directed
- tell what the book does
- identify some unique feature about the book or author
- briefly identify the competition

In phrasing your introductory section, you want to show the editor that you know what you are talking about, that you have a realistic idea of the market, and that you are not billing your book as the end-all publishing. The tables on pages 41 and 42 show some common errors that neophytes make in their proposals and prospectuses and the correct way to present the information. In item 1 on page 41, the prospective author shows he does not know the realities of college textbook publishing. No book is right for all these courses. Instead, the audience should be clearly identified, as it is in the "Good" column, so the editor will know at once whether the proposed book is in an area for which he or she is looking to acquire a book. In item 2, the author is disregarding too lightly a competing book. Even if he hates the book, the fact that others are using it, and in large quantities, indicates it must have something going for it. It is the prospective author's job to find what that something is and to identify it in the prospectus. In item 3 of the same table, the problem is again lack of specificity and grandiosity. No book just *is* better – if it has better features than the competition, they have to be identified.

Table 2.2 / Phrasing Your Prospectus

Poor	Good
(1) This book can be used in any business course, from Introduction to Business Management to Advanced Business Law, since it covers all aspects of business.	The proposed text is designed for use in courses generally called "Introduction to Business Management" or "Business Management-I"
(2) The Leahy text with which this book competes is terrible and no instructor in his or her right mind could possibly prefer it to my book.	The major strength of the Leahy book, a traditional leader in the market, is its emphasis on practical business methods, but it is considered weak in its handling of research applications. In the proposed text, I have attempted to emulate Leahy's practical orientation, but at the same time to include more research.
(3) My book covers all topics more thoroughly and better than any other book available.	The proposed text is designed specifically for the community college and "soft" four-year college market, which favors an eclectic approach over the analytical. This is why Jessup's book is currently the leader in the community college market, while Singh's and McCarthy's are leaders in the "hard" courses of the four-year market.

In Table 2.3 we look at some proposal material for a book on the insurance industry. Since there have been many books written about the less ethical side of the business, the poor version of (1) shows that the writer is not aware of the other books that he should be familiar with, while the good version shows that he recognizes other books and knows how his book differs from these others. In (2) the poor approach generalizes with overly melodramatic and non-specific language what is to come, while the good approach stresses some specific information that is going to be discussed in the book. In (3) the tendency toward hyperbole and grandiosity is not nearly as powerful as the specific credentials and credibility of the author as an authority on the subject—a person eminently capable of exposing frauds.

Table 2.3 / Phrasing Your Trade Book Proposal

Poor	Good
(1) There has never been an expose of the insurance industry that reveals it for what it really is, without mincing words and with all its blemishes intact or even highlighted.	While there have been a number of books written critical of the insurance business, this one is written from an insider's perspective, backed by five years of intensive research.
(2) The book will reveal all the seamy side of the insurance business: a side that will shock many who think of insurance as safety for their future.	I will discuss in detail the Colorado Insurance Co. fraud in which ten thousand policy holders lost their equity, as well as the failure of regulating agencies in most states to keep track of what is actually going on in the companies.
(3) This book can easily become another classic of muckraking, having an impact such as *The Jungle* did on the meat packing industry or Ralph Nader's *Unsafe at Any Speed* had on the car industry.	The author, a prominent figure in the insurance industry until his retirement last year has crusaded for three decades for better insurance practices and has been instrumental in exposing some of the major insurance frauds of the past forty years.

(3) Competing and Compatible Titles. This section is extremely important in textbook prospectuses, but not always as important in a proposal for a trade book. It depends on the amount of competition and how directly your book will compete. Listing and critically discussing the competing books does two things: it shows the editor you are familiar with the market, and it shows him or her you have studied the competition, that you know the strengths and weaknesses of your book as opposed to "theirs." Notice how the specific comments in section (3) inform the editor of your thorough familiarity with the competition.

Notice that in the text prospectus only three books are listed. There are dozens of titles in this field, so why did the authors choose to list these three particular titles? Two criteria narrowed down the choice. First, they chose texts that sell reasonably well or very well. No editor wants to bring out a title to compete with books that have failed in the marketplace. Second, they chose texts that were on a level similar to their proposed text, neither too "soft" nor geared for more advanced students at better schools.

In the trade book proposal, you will notice there are no competing titles listed. This does not mean that *How to Start and Run Your Own Word Processing Business* is the only book of its type, although I would like to believe it is the best. Rather, the absence of competing titles means that the proposed book is not competing for consumer purchase directly with other comparable titles. In fact, a person thinking of going into such a business might reasonably purchase several such books to help him or her in getting started. Instead of competing with other books, then, the proposed book is vying for a *specific audience,* and that audience is clearly identified in the proposal, right at the beginning. Competing titles may be eliminated from a trade book proposal if the audience (market) is more a critical factor than the competing titles or if there are so many other prominent titles that it is assumed the editor would be familiar with them.

There is an alternative to listing competing titles, one that is highly effective in getting the attention of an editor, but which requires a lot of work since you have to assemble it separately for each publisher. But it may well be worth the trouble in the long run. I call it Compatible Titles. A brief example is found in this section of the trade book proposal, where I pointed out that the proposed book would fit nicely into a series the publisher has in print. Two other examples illustrate what this approach does and why it is important:

Text Example—*An Introduction to Health*

> The Blankety/Blank Publishing house is ideally suited to publish this kind of book. Your current titles in Drug Education (Byrne, *Adolescent Drug Abuse;* and Howman/Ketter/Vance, *Drug Education for Teachers*), in human sexuality (Grassmere's *Human Sexuality: An Introduction*), and in Nursing (Tallis and Zanderwald's *Introduction to Nursing*) circumscribe the market for this kind of text. The proposed text, *Introduction to Health,* can serve as an important lead-in for your company's sales reps when visiting physical education, nursing, community health, and home economics departments where these courses are taught.

Trade Example — *How to Quiet Your Mother-in-Law*

> The proposed book, How to Quiet Your Mother-in-Law
> would seem to fit in perfectly with your series, "Getting
> Rid of Relatives You Hate." I have personally found the
> titles on sister's-in-law, father's, and step-siblings most
> helpful, and wondered why no book on mothers-in-law
> was included. The current project is developed around
> the outline common to the books in the series. I think it
> would fit in nicely, and it could be marketed with the
> other titles.

You can see from these two examples that what the "compatible titles" device essentially does is to show an editor how your title would fit into a publisher's list. This, naturally, differs from publisher to publisher, but rarely is there an editor who will not be impressed by your ability to pinpoint the market and to show how that market already enjoys some penetration by his or her publishing house. You can, by the way, easily find out this information simply by sending for and maintaining a file of catalogues from publishing companies. These will be useful on many occasions, so it is a good idea to maintain an up-to-date file of current catalogues, many of which also include forthcoming publications.

Another way of showing the editor you are aware of the potential market and previously successful efforts is through what I call "name dropping." Here, you allude to another author or work that has made a mark in the same way you intend to.

> The proposed book, with its emphasis on technological
> changes in the work place, can prove to be another *Elec-*
> *tronic Cottage* or *Megatrends*. Like those two other works,
> the author brings to bear on the question of future
> changes in the workplace a background of technical ex-
> pertise, consulting, and managerial experience.

One must be cautious in using this technique, however, not to exaggerate, and not to lose touch with the realistic value of one's work. Not every career decision book is another *What Color is Your Parachute?*, just as not every new book about nineteenth-century Georgia can be compared with *Gone With the Wind*.

(4) Unique Features and Pedagogical Aids. In these sections, which may or may not be identified by separate headings, you elaborate the unique features you alluded to briefly in the introduction. These features should differentiate your proposed book in a positive way from other books available. Follow the advice in the tables on pages 41-42 about the correct ways to phrase your unique features.

Unique features generally include any of the following, depending on the type of book and the features of the competing books.

- A thematic emphasis, especially a synthesis
- A practical orientation or many examples
- A new or previously unidentified market
- More detailed coverage

In many proposals, the unique features are discussed in some other section. In our sample prospectus, which includes separate headings for "Pedagogical Aids" and "Special Topics Covered," it was decided that another heading for unique features would detract from the overall continuity and thematic unity of the prospectus. So, what are actually some of the book's unique features—its "attempt to synthesize research findings and theoretical frameworks to show . . . the continuing impact of socialization over the course of life. . . ."—are indicated in the section on competing titles.

In the sample trade book proposal, the unique features are scattered throughout the introduction. It was not necessary to have a section on unique features isolated here, since the book was not designed to compete directly with other books on the same subject. Since the entire tone and content of this book differentiated it from others, no special emphasis on unique features was used, although these were indicated in the content of the proposal.

Two special instances may demand particular attention. First, most textbooks, especially for precollege levels (el/hi) and for large, introductory undergraduate courses, rely heavily on pedagogical features. These features help the teacher use the book effectively in the course and motivate students to learn. It is important, in developing your prospectus, to know what kinds of features have been employed successfully in the competing titles in your subject matter area, and to then include as many of them as possible in yours. Some of the more common (and important) features are:

- Outlines and summaries preceding and following the chapters.
- An effective art program. This can be a big boon, especially for an introductory level text.
- An instructor's manual and test bank. Both of these, if well prepared, are inducements for instructors to adopt the text, since these assist their efforts at teaching the course.
- Practical examples with which students can identify.
- Annotated bibliographies, glossaries, and marginal notes.

Second, certain types of trade books benefit greatly from practical features—the trade book equivalent of pedagogical aids. A book on preparing your income taxes, for example, would benefit from fill-in charts and diagrams that allow the reader different ways of computing taxes. This book – *Getting Published: A Guide for Business People & Other Professionals* – benefits from the elaboration of writing methods and the practical exercises I have used at seminars – and these features were clearly mentioned in the proposal I submitted to the publisher. Many books benefit from self-assessment questionnaires and exercises that allow the reader to participate more fully in the process, or case histories, personal anecdotes, illustrations or charts and diagrams.

(5) Special Topics Covered. In textbooks especially, "hot" topics in the field – from sociobiology to zero-based budgeting and management by objectives – are often the critical reason why one book does better than another. High school textbook committees and college professors are always on the lookout for at least some inclusion of the new topics they consider important.

"Special topics" do not really have to be special. They may be the same topics covered in other recent books that have proved successful in the market; in fact, they usually are. But when you list them in your prospectus, it shows the editor and reviewer you know they are important and indicates that you are giving these topics the special attention they deserve. This section of your prospectus, more than any of the others, characterizes your book as either current or old-fashioned, in step with the times or anachronistic. So be sure you know what topics are special and that you indicate them there.

How do you find out what are considered the most important topics? Textbook publishers typically rely on feedback reports from their field representatives and on professionally prepared market research, which has gained increasing importance in textbook development.

Still, without the benefit of a cadre of field reps or expensive market research in hand, there is a very simple way for *you* to get this information. Just look carefully over the brochures and advertisements that publishers of the competing titles have put out. These are sent free on request by writing to the publisher. Also, look through the professional journals where their ads appear. Notice the way they are promoting their new books and which features they emphasize. Most likely they have done the work for you, and what they are touting about their new book is what you should be including in your prospectus.

Thumbing through the professional journals where these books are advertised is not only the best way to see which features the marketing department of the other publishing companies have deemed most important, but also to see the topics that will be important in the next generation of titles. This can put you one step ahead of the competition, especially where the inclusion or exclusion of topics in a discipline changes rapidly (data processing and biology are two examples).

In the trade proposal, the familiarity of the names of the computers, word processors, and software becomes the "special topic covered."

(6) Brief Table of Contents and (7) Detailed Outline. Always include in your prospectus a brief (preferably one-page) table of contents that an editor can glance at rapidly before reading a detailed outline. This provides the editor or reviewer with a swift understanding of the scope of your project against which the detailed outline can be measured.

Avoid catchy title chapters unless they are accompanied by explanatory titles. Use the same rules of exactitude you followed in selecting a tentative title for the book.

Wrong

The Riddle of the Sphinx (Psychology Text)
A Yen for Success! (Management Text)
Pumping Iron (Biology Text)

Right

The Riddle of the Sphinx: Development Over the Lifespan
The Japanese Way of Doing Business: Yen for Success
The Heart and Circulatory System: Pumping Iron

The purpose of the brief table of contents is to inform the project reviewer about the general scope and organization of the book. It provides a context for evaluating the detailed outline.

Many prospective authors agonize unnecessarily when creating the detailed outline. Remember, the detailed outline is not a finished product; it is only a *suggested* outline.

In fact, the majority of text books as they are developed and reviewed through various stages, undergo so many changes in structure, content, and scope that there is often little similarity between the detailed outline of the prospectus and the final table of contents in the published book. I can recall very few occasions in my own experience where the outline accurately predicted what the final book would look like.

(8) Section Overviews. A section overview is one possible way to help the reviewer understand why the book is being organized in the way it is. You may also place a running short outline against the longer outline to accomplish this. In both cases, what you are trying to do is show how you are managing the project, what you're using as your organizing theme or principle.

In our sample text book prospectus, we see that the four main parts of the book mirror the way these courses are typically divided. This, of course, is clear on the short outline; but since the reviewer may be paying careful attention to the longer outline, he or she may forget how the parts relate to the whole and it is the purpose of these section heads to make that clear.

If you have an effective writing style, or if the style or level of your proposed book is important, a sample chapter can be a big plus. Editors are constantly wary of the technician or expert who claims in the book proposal to be able to speak comfortably to the lay person in his or her own language, but who in fact is so used to the gobbledygook of the profession that it is all but impossible to even think in terms that other people can understand. What the editor will want to see is an example of how you can write – *in practice,* rather than theory – at the level the book is presumably intended.

Many times the expert has a plethora of ideas but lacks the ability to translate them to the printed page. Editors are often willing to pair the expert with a professional writer, who can hone the ideas into good prose. But it is only with some sample material that the editor can make this type of determination.

Principles of an Effective Proposal or Prospectus

Various disciplines and various situations may require special types of prospectuses. Every field, moreover, has its own buzz words and inside perspectives. But the main points we have suggested throughout this chapter should, when employed properly, augur well for an effective textbook prospectus or trade book proposal. Summing up these main points, we can say:

1. The proposal/prospectus should identify the *scope* of the proposed project, its potential *market,* its main *competition,* and its unique *features.*

2. The *approach, philosophy, style,* and *attitude* of the author, both with regard to the subject matter, to the most popular books in the field, and to the writing task itself, should be revealed through the proposal/prospectus.

3. The language used should be *precise.* It must do two things at the same time: *sell the idea* of the project and show that *you* are the person to carry it through. In a trade book proposal, it is also helpful to indicate what special qualities or affiliations you have that may help sell the book.

3

Getting It on Paper

The average book takes anywhere from one to three years to write. The average journal article takes anywhere from six months to a year, although many authors argue that this is only the final writing, and that the development of the ideas takes much longer. These estimates include the time taken for the extensive amount of library research and literature review that might precede the writing, the various stages of draft preparation, reviewer feedback, and final rewriting. In other words, writing for publication is usually a very time-consuming endeavor.

Yet it is often possible to do just as fine a job in about half the time. Writers who write for a living know that in order to survive they cannot afford the luxury of wasting time indulged in by the amateur. Many technical writers in science, business, and health churn out 3 or 4 excellent articles a year. The neophyte writer, laboring slowly and painfully for years over his or her *magnum opus,* imbuing the prose with rich phrases that only time-consuming deliberation and reworking can provide, would do well to remember that such great phrase makers as Dostoyevsky, H.L. Mencken, Mark Twain, and Charles Dickens all wrote their best works under strict deadlines.

The key to fast and effective publishable writing is what I call *time budgeting*—a system of organization and writing that has demonstrated results for dozens of individuals working on projects ranging from short papers for in-house journals to lengthy doctoral dissertations, and even for full-length college level textbooks. One of the things we will do in the following pages is focus on using time budgeting to get started on the project.

In this chapter, four concrete stages of writing for publication are covered, with some real examples from various professions and target audiences. These stages are based on the types of practical problems that prospective authors encounter, beginning with their inveterate procrastination (which prevents about 90% of them from getting anything done) to the typical quagmire of hopelessly scattered notes and forgotten ideas. The four stages are:

1. overcoming procrastination
2. setting up a regular working schedule
3. writing in "chunks"
4. constructively using reviewers' feedback and editors' suggestions, along with your own good judgment as you work.

In addition, two methods of writing that I have used successfully in my workshops and in my own writing endeavors are discussed. One method, called the *3-page method,* is a quick way of developing a project of any length while never working on more than three pages at a time. It narrows down a big task to its minimal components and helps the prospective writer overcome the key cause of writing procrastination—that the *whole task* as it lies ahead appears too formidable and imposing at the outset. This same psychological principle of breaking down the whole into smaller parts is the basis for another method, discussed later, called *writing in chunks.*

These principles and methods are demonstrated in the actual construction of a journal article that you will see develop, stage by stage, in the pages of this book. This "real" example helps you see how this system can be implemented to accomplish tangible results.

Budgeting Your Time

It is essential that you budget your time at the beginning of a project. This enables you to overcome any tendencies toward procrastination and to set up a regular working schedule that will assure continued progress.

Getting started on your project includes three basic phases: (1) defining the scope of the project and its market (audience); (2) allocating your initial research time and correspondence/prospectus writing time; (3) reassessing the project before working on it by using preliminary publisher/editor feedback.

The previous chapter reviewed what you *should* do in your prospectus, where you evaluate the merits of your ideas. In this section the focus is on how to get started actually outlining your article or prospectus—how to set the time aside, budget it, and begin to use it most fully.

If Only I Had The Time

In my experiences with prospective writers, I have consistently found the single reason most often cited to explain why the would-be writer hasn't been able to get started is a lack of time. "If only I had the time," is the rejoinder I get time and again to my inquiries about why a project that sounds so good has gone by the wayside. "I've been so damn busy lately that I literally haven't had a second to work on the article."

Probably true. But in fact, the only people who really have enough time to write are likely to have nothing useful to write about. Yet good writing does get done, and by people who apparently don't have the time. Why? How? When?

EXERCISE

"I Wish I Had Time to Write"

If you believe you haven't had the time to get started on your writing project, that you've just been too busy, write on the lines below as honestly as you can, how many minutes you estimate you spent in the past week on each of the following activities:

Talking on the phone to friends _____
Watching a sporting event _____
Watching the evening new _____
Watching other TV _____
Attending a play or movie _____
Browsing, shopping, or beauty/health/exercise _____
Tennis, Racquet ball, or other sports _____
Traveling on public transportation _____
Eating out _____
Visiting friends _____
Reading for pleasure _____

Add up the minutes and you have an idea of how much time you can set aside regularly, if you really want to, for your writing ambitions. It may mean that you have to give up some of your reading, limit talking on the phone, cancel a visit to the hair stylist or exercise club, or that you have to jot down your writing notes while commuting in the morning. But it means too that if you *can* set aside x minutes per week, that those x minutes will add up to hours, then to pages, and then to a completed project.

The Time-Budgeting Technique

If writing is important to you, would you be willing to set aside 3% of your time for the task? If so, this works out to a commitment of about five hours a week, and certainly you can afford that. In fact, if you put a real five hours per week into writing – and by "real," I mean without distractions – you will be astonished at how much you can get done in a month.

But you can't just say, "OK, I'm willing to give it five hours." This won't work. You will always find something more important than writing to do at any given time. Sure, you tell yourself you can write later on, but right now you simply must do – – –. You can fill in the blanks with your own pet time-fillers. Here are a few common things that are more important than writing at any given moment.

- Do the laundry
- Call mom, whom you haven't called yet this week
- Play with the kids
- Finish that great novel you started reading
- Wax the kitchen floor
- Bring the car in for an oil change
- Go to the library
- Go to the dry cleaner
- Buy a new suit for Jay's Bar Mitzvah
- Pour some drano down the bath drain
- Paint the foyer

All of these are important, to be sure, And, in my experience, any one will win over writing any time with the rationalization, "I'll get that writing done later." And later becomes later, and later. . .

The time budgeting technique resolves this problem forever. It is a simple technique that works like this: First, you decide how many hours *this* week you want to devote to writing. For this example, I use five hours, but you may chose anywhere between three and ten hours. Less than three hours will not be sufficiently productive, and you should try to succeed in shorter exercises before you attempt more than ten hours per week.

> *STEP ONE:* This week between *Sunday, July 8th at 9 pm* and *Sunday, July 15th at 9 pm* I will spend *five* hours working on my article, *"Sexual Exclusivity: An Ideal or Illogical Idea."*

Notice that I have clearly and specifically defined the period of time (day, month, hour), the exact number of hours I will spend, and the name of the project on which I will work. With this, I have made a preliminary commitment to getting to work.

The next step further breaks down the formidable whole into manageable parts. You allocate your time into segments. As a minimum,

I recommend 45 minutes per segment; as a maximum, 2 hours. Much depends on your powers of concentration, on your schedule, and on how long it takes you to get moving once you sit down with your pen or typewriter. Again, it is important to be specific.

> *STEP TWO:* These *five* hours will be divided into five *one-hour* periods. — or — These *five* hours will be divided into two *two-hour* sessions and one *one-hour* session.

The third step is the most critical – and most difficult. Here you must do two things. First you have to identify (reserve) the specific times of the week when you will be working. This sets aside your writing time so that you will not find something more important to do, such as the activities indicated on our foregoing list of "more-important-things-to-do-right-now."

Second – and here is where behavorial psychology comes in – you have to pair each segment of writing time with some contingent event; a reward that you will get when you complete the segment. And that reward should follow immediately *after* the writing time. This is called proximate reinforcement, and it is a powerful tool in shaping behavior.

As rigid as this sounds, it has worked marvelously even for the most intransigent procrastinators. If you have trouble doing this spontaneously, make a chart (like the one below) of the five or six most enjoyable activities of the week ahead – the things you are actually looking forward to this week – and indicate the time of each. Reserve the time immediately before those activities for your writing.

Time	Enjoyable Activities
Every night from 11 to 11:30	Watching the news on TV before going to bed
This Wednesday at noon	Lunch with Mr. Charles, who will sign a big contract
Sunday afternoon	Watching the Red Sox game next Sunday

> *STEP THREE:* 1. I will work at home on Monday evening, July 9th, between *10 and 11 o'clock*, after which I may watch the evening news.   *Writing time: 1 Hour*
>
> 2. I will work on Wednesday in my office from *11 to 1 pm*, immediately before my lunch date with Mr. Charles.

I will tell the secretary absolutely no calls are to be put through at that time.   *Writing time: 2 Hrs.*

3. I will work on Sunday, the 15th from *11 am to 1 pm,* immediately before the Red Sox game, which I will not watch if I have not done my work. *Writing time: 2 hrs.*

You have now set aside your time reserved for writing only, and will be rewarded immediately after working by the pleasurable activity you have made contingent on that work. There are a few rules you have to obey during this writing-only time in order for the time budgeting technique to work as effectively as it should. While some people may require special rules and restrictions for success, the following are the ones most common needed.

Rules to Be Followed During Writing Time
1. No telephone calls, no interruptions – none!

2. No reading and a minimum of reviewing of notes and ideas, all of which can be done before. It's very easy to use about 40% of your writing time for thinking, but writing time is for the actual physical act of writing. The pen should be kept moving or the typewriter keys pounding for as much of the time as is possible.

3. Stay in the place you have set aside for writing. If you have to go to the bathroom, be sure to go and return without discussion along the way. There is no time more tempting for chatting with one's spouse or colleague than when one has to write.

4. Do no other work, except for "warm-up," which is discussed later. This is not the time to finish that letter you began last week. You are obligated to work only on what you said you would work on.

Now, with the time set aside and the rules understood, you are ready to get down to work, ready at last to translate your ideas into written form.

The 3-Page Method

Generally, after the big obstacle of procrastination has been overcome, a second obstacle arises, bringing an equally countervailing force to bear on the progress of work. "How will I ever complete such a monumental project?" the prospective writer asks in trepidation. "Am I perhaps taking on a lot more than I can handle?" Who am I, after all, to write about his important subject? Where do I begin?" Even if the task is really not monumental – and it usually isn't – the very thought of embarking on the project might be enough to discourage all but the bravest souls. The classic picture of the doctoral candidate unable to complete a dissertation year after year, despite the work already put into it, reflects what I have found to be a characteristic in all areas of writing endeavors: feeling overwhelmed by the prospect of what lies ahead.

As with time budgeting, our strategy here is to break down a seemingly massive task into small, manageable parts, each of which the prospective writer realizes is within his or her reach. In fact, this technique makes it so simple, that when many people first hear about it, they laugh apprehensively, quite sure it won't work.

The 3-page method actually begins with three blank pages, which we call 1, 2, and 3.

1	2	3

Our basic assumption is that what actually frightens most people about working on a writing project are the myriad creative options and logical possibilities, combined with the total lack of direction that they face when they try to write. The following exercise shows how the problem can be resolved.

EXERCISE

The 3-Page Method

Take three sheets of writing paper and number them 1, 2, 3. On page 1 print your tentative title, even if it is just a vague working title. On this page you then create, in seventy-five words or less (preferably less), your opening paragraph. Instead of a paragraph, you may create your opening two sentences. But no more than seventy-five words – that's important.

You have just made a great start with less than seventy-five words!

On Page 2 you also write less than seventy-five words. List two or three important things that you article will say. These do not have to be well-written; what is important is that you have some good ideas. If you don't have two or three good ideas, examples, insights, or observations – well, perhaps you should reconsider your topic and maybe choose another one.

You have just made tremendous progress with fewer than a total of 150 words. Read on!

On Page 3, you also work with less than seventy-five words. Here you should have some fun. Without writing a word of your "real" article, you are to imagine how you will conclude your article. Write a concluding paragraph or some concluding sentences in less than seventy-five words. How can you possibly know this? One hint is your end paragraph and your opening paragraph are likely to be very similar.

Congratulations! You are going to get that article done after all!

You will see this method at work in the following pages as I develop in front of you a real article that I am currently working on, hoping to read at a professional convention. This article is geared for a professional journal in the marriage and family counseling field. It is intended for the type of journal read by marriage counselors, psychologists, and academicians. The article evolved from some lectures I gave in a graduate course on marital relationships. I thought it might be a good idea to publish some of these observations since I had done a lot of research and the students found them quite interesting, but for months I hadn't been able to find the time to get around to it. You see, I put things off too!

You might go along with these examples and begin putting *your* ideas into shape *now,* using this method. That, in fact, would be far better than procrastinating more by saying, "I'll read through the book first and then come back and do this."

1

Title: "Sexual Exclusivity: An Ideal or 'Illogical Idea'?"

Opening: Across all Western cultures, the institutions of marriage has always been intricately entwined with the concept of sexual exclusivity. Through religious sanctions, family pressures, economic constraints, customs and laws, marriage presupposes that each partner will maintain relations with and only with the spouse. Extension of this rule includes engagement relationships, cohabitational relationships, and other so-called "serious" relationships that precede the marriage vows.

2

Main Points to Be Covered: (1) There is no longer a rational or scientific basis to require sexually exclusive relationships. (2) There is considerable research that the majority of marital relationships are no longer sexually exclusive, even though they are made to appear so through deceptions. (3) The idea of exclusivity goes back to old religious roots and property laws that largely discriminate against women. The principle of exclusivity still results in a "double standard" that discriminates against women.

3

Concluding Paragraph: We have seen, then, that although the idea of sexual exclusivity still permeates our thinking about successful cohabitational and marital relationships, there is little rational basis for holding on to this value. On the contrary, since it is statistically becoming less and less the norm, there is some good reason to abandon it. In the rational-emotive theory of Albert Ellis, this concept represents an "illogical idea," one that we have been propagandized as children to believe in. Such ideas, we note, almost always serve some purpose. In this case the purpose is twofold: first, to allow people of less maturity to enter comfortably into marital relationships; and second, to keep marriage compatible with and supported by inflexible religious institutions.

In less than 250 words, I now have a beginning, and outline, and an end for my article. I might even put it away until the next writing-only time slot and then continue with the second part. There is no need to push yourself, to force out ideas. With this method, stage by stage, the writing will come naturally.

Second-Stage – The 3-Page Method

Again, we begin with three blank pages, this time numbering them 1a, 2a, and 3a to differentiate them from the earlier draft. You might even use paper of a different color. Keep the previous stage on your desk, since you will be using it here.

On page 1a, in seventy-five words or less, write one complete paragraph introducing your idea 1 from page 2 of the previous stage. For example, I would take my idea 1, "There is no longer a logical basis to require sexually exclusive relationships," and develop it into a paragraph of three or four sentences to show *why* there is no longer a logical basis, why there once was, or how that basis has disappeared. Remember, you are only being asked to write a single introductory paragraph here, not a complete exposition of the idea.

1a	2a	3a
IDEA #1	IDEA #2 A B C	CONC. PARA.

Next, on page 2a, you list – again, in seventy-five words or less – three points, ideas, references, sentences, observations, examples, or insights about your idea 2 from page 2 of the previous exercise. I might support my statement, "There is considerable research . . ." with some specific studies. I could list the studies and summarize in a few words, or show with some statistical data, the main findings. Since this is only the beginning of the supportive development, I need not worry about being too exact or thorough at this point.

On page 3a, rewrite your concluding paragraph from the previous page 3 to be sure it now includes an accurate summary of the material that has emerged in your development of ideas 1 and 2 on pages 1a and 2a. Each new stage of the 3-page exercise expands the work of the previous stage, generating new paragraphs and new drafts of previously-developed paragraphs. Over time, this leads to a complete, final draft of a chapter or of an article. Table 3.2 suggests one possible sequence of stages. Some individuals who have learned to use this method have altered the sequence to conform to their specialized needs and time limitations. Also, after using this method for a while it may evolve into a natural way of organizing your writing time, so that you will be able to deviate from it freely without disrupting the progress of your work.

Writing in Chunks

The 3-page method is an application of a more general approach that I call *writing in chunks*. A chunk may be a skeleton outline section, a sentence or two, a paragraph, or even part of a chapter. I have found that for me, but not for everyone, writing progresses smoothly when I divide the whole into small parts, as in the 3-page method. But there is another underlying principle here, also worthy of attention and analysis. Notice that when you use the 3-page method, in each writing session the time is divided between working on *new* material and rewriting *old* material into newer drafts. In effect, by doing this you are apportioning your time and mental energy between bursts of creating something out of nothing and the craft of fine-tuning the prose you've already jotted down. This might

Table 3.1

GENERATING A FULL ARTICLE
BY THE 3-PAGE METHOD

	Stage 1	Stage 2	Stage 3	Stage 4	Stage 5	Stage 6	Stage 7	Stage 8	Stage 9
Pgs:	1	1a	1b	1c	1d	1e	1f	1g	1h
	2	2a	2b	2c	2d	2e	2f	2g	2h
	3	3a	3b	3c	3d	3e	3f	3g	3h
Approx. Total Words	200	350	500	650	800	950	1100	1250	1400
Approx. Complete Paragraphs	½	1	2	3	5	7	9	11	13
Approx. Time in Hours	1.5	3	4.5	6	7.5	9	10.5	12	13.5
% of Total 15-Page Article	–	1%	3%	6%	10%	15%	20%	25%	35%

seem like a fine distinction, but I find that most people's creative well-spring decreases to a trickle in a relatively short time and that using the additional writing time to rework material allows a replenishing of the well while watering the garden.

I distinguish between two fundamentally different kinds of chunks: *germinal* chunks and *terminal* chunks. A germinal chunk is a sentence like the preceding one: it serves as the germ for further development. A germinal chunk cannot stand as is, but cries out for further development, for some exposition. It might be the topic sentence of a paragraph or a statement in a skeleton outline. Such a chunk ineluctably leads to other chunks, of which the final ones are the terminal chunks. These terminal chunks predominate as you complete your ideas, paragraphs, and sections, drawing them to their expository end. Terminal chunks are the reward for your labors and can be identified by their finality as sentences. Like this one. Or the preceding one.

A third type of chunk – I call it a *warm up* chunk – is just as important for some writers, although not quite as relevant to the end-product. Many writers, from the inexperienced to the famous, require certain ritual behaviors each day before getting started on their work. Hemingway would sharpen all his pencils before putting down his first word on paper. Henry Miller used to write five or six letters before he could get started on his real work for the day. Some writers have to use the bathroom before working, looking over their notes and reviewing their day's plans while relieving their bowels. One friend of mine has to sing an aria from Wagner – loudly! – before beginning writing his book on biology. Psychologists can worry about why these strange behaviors evolved and what they mean: our job is to help you get started.

A warm up chunk is designed for those of you who have not already discovered an effective pre-writing ritual, such as those described above. If you have difficulty getting down to work each day and no ritual to make the getting there easier, this kind of chunk should help you get started for the day.

A warm up chunk should have some relevance to the project you are working on, or at least to your professional life in general, but sometimes it may not. Whatever works, works! I have consistently found that a warm up chunk works best when it has been custom-tailored for the person using it. These are a few examples that have been employed successfully, but you might want to create your own, to suit your own needs and interests. The important thing is that it should involve some actual writing – that is, getting the psycho-motor coordination and thought processes chugging along.

Some Suggested Warm-Up Chunks

1. Write a paragraph of two of a glowing review of your book or article, pointing out what a monumental contribution it is to the profession,

Table 3.2

STAGES OF THE 3-PAGE METHOD

Opening paragraph	Stage 1
Ideas #1, #2, #3	
Concluding paragraph	
Idea #1, opening paragraph	Stage 2
Idea #2, #3, new sentences	
Concluding paragraph (rev.)	
Idea #2, opening paragraph	Stage 3
Idea #3, new sentences	
Concluding paragraph (rev.)	
Idea #3, opening paragraph	Stage 4
Idea #1, opening paragraph	
Idea #2, opening paragraph	
Divide paragraph 1 into three paragraphs	Stage 5
Paragraph #1-1	
Paragraph #1-2	
Paragraph #1-3	
Divide paragraph 2 into three paragraphs	Stage 6
Paragraph #2-1	
Paragraph #2-2	
Paragraph #2-3	
Divide paragraph 3 into three paragraphs	Stage 7
Paragraph #3-1	
Paragraph #3-2	
Paragraph #3-3	
Opening paragraph (rev.)	Stage 8
Paragraph #1-1 (rev.)	
Concluding Paragraph (rev.)	

Note: The sequence may be altered if there are more than three main ideas for development. But the basic progression remains, whereby each idea ultimately becomes three separate paragraphs. After all ideas have been broken down into paragraphs, a new opening and concluding paragraph is created. This sequence is repeated until article is done.

how brilliantly you achieved your goals, etc. Avoid any hints of modesty.

2. Make a list of obligations and chores you have to do today and tomorrow that are actually unpleasant enough that you prefer writing to doing any of them.

3. Discuss briefly what project or projects you would hope to undertake when the one you are working on now is completed.

The Shoulders of Others

Almost every great writer, and all of us lesser souls, depend at times upon the wise judgment of others to improve our works, especially where our vision is distorted by our emotional investment, by philosophical or perceptual rigidity, or by an overinvolvement with the writing process that prevents us from sufficiently distancing ourselves from the final product. Although I might agree with Alexander Pope's assessment of criticism in general—"Tis hard to say, if greater want of skill-Appear in writing or in judging ill"—I have still found the criticism of others invaluable in the development of all my writings. And like Sir Isaac Newton, who wrote, "If I have seen further, it is by standing upon the shoulder of Giants," I recognize that many of my better perceptions and more successful writings were made possible only by the prescient viewpoints of others, who shared their knowledge with me.

Unfortunately, most of us will not have giants on whose shoulders we can stand. Midgets are more often the rule. But still, even the slightest of judges will sometimes reveal to us truths that, when incorporated and weighed by an open and dispassionate intellect, can blossom into important constructive changes in the final writing product.

There are three principles I have found in soliciting and using the advice and criticism of others. The first rule, the most important and yet the most difficult for many, is to put aside your ego, disassociate yourself emotionally from your work, accept that *you* as a person can be valuable, important and loved—even if someone has something negative to say about your work.

This is, unfortunately, easier said than done. I will never forget when a client of mine called me, nearly in tears, devastated by a letter he had just received from a prospective agent he had asked to represent his new book. "The agent hated it," he told me, "thought it a worthless piece of crap. I really have to agree, after thinking about it. He's right, you know. I don't think I can go on with this."

I couldn't imagine what terrible things the agent had written to upset him so. You can imagine my surprise when I read the agent's letter and found not only was it not discouraging, but it was even somewhat enthusiastic about the project. The agent had merely suggested some additional work to improve the publishing prospects.

I realized then that this person's ego was so fragile that only the most unrestrained and bombastic praise, free of even the slightest suggestions for change, could make him feel someone really liked his book.

Of course, most of us are not so vulnerable emotionally. Still, most of us are hurt when our work is picked apart. When words at which we worked so hard are pruned, it is sometimes like having a part of yourself mutilated. If you close yourself off to criticism because of your ego, however, you are losing a valuable source of information that can help you improve and grow as a writer.

The second rule, in a way, is almost a parallel of the first, but likely to apply to a different type of person. Don't be too willing to listen to criticism. Don't accept everything critics tell you. Don't be too open.

You have to strike a balance between your own independent judgment and what others tell you. This might be called the constructive mean of criticism.

I remember one instance where I had the outline for what I thought an innovative book of readings in educational psychology. The selections were original, dramatic, informative — selections from literature, theater, and philosophy that I thought students would love to read. I had even field-tested the material in my classes with great success.

But my editor at the publishing house suggested I cut out certain articles and add a few educational and psychological studies he thought helpful. I accepted his suggestions without sufficient thought, since he had been so consistently correct in his judgments about the book on which I worked with him before. But as it turned out he was wrong here, completely wrong, and had I the sense to maintain my independent judgment I would have seen this at the time and my book would have been much more successful.

The third rule: select the right reviewers. This has many implications. Don't ask your husband, wife, or lover to be your primary reviewer: they are bound to let too many feelings, positive or negative, get in the way. On a less obvious level, you have to select a reader/reviewer whose point of view will be sympathetic to the project. Or, at least one who can be objective from another point of view.

Imagine an ardent behavioral psychologist reviewing a new book on Freudian psychoanalysis. What would you expect? Or, can you see *The New York Review of Books* reviewing the latest Harold Robbins bestseller, or *Mademoiselle* recommending to its readers the latest work in phenomenological philosophy? The interest and point of view of the reviewer brings a lot to bear on what he or she finally concludes. While you want someone who will not be opposed to your point of view at the outset, you also want someone who will not be so agreeable and easy to please that the criticism of others will not be anticipated.

Putting these rules and observations together, you can see that intelligent and well-selected review and criticism are important stages in the development of a writing project, that every project gets some negative comments, and that if these negative comments and constructive suggestions are wisely but selectively incorporated, the final product will be significantly improved.

4

Finding a Publisher

How would you answer the following questions?

1. How many magazines and journals are published regularly in the United States and Canada?

a.   1,500   b.   3,000
c. 15,000   d. 50,000
e. 65,000

2. How many people in the United States have had at least one article or book published in the past year?

a.   5,000   b. 20,000
c. 10,000   d. 80,000
e. 160,000

3. How many professional associations are there in the United States and what percentage of them publish a newsletter, magazine, or some other regular publication?

a. over 3,000   b. over 12,000
c. over 6,000   d. over 24,000
e. over 48,000

The correct choice is (e) for all of them. If you've answered all three questions correctly, then you already realize the enormous opportunities for publication. You realize too that there is a short supply of good material around, not nearly enough to fill up all the blank pages available, and that if you have something of value to offer, you have an excellent chance of seeing it published. Editors at book publishing houses and at magazines are constantly scouting for good material from professional people, from experts and consultants, and from teachers who can express their knowledge and teaching ability in print.

But possibly, even recognizing this situation in the abstract, you still do not know the right way to find the best publisher for *your* work. If you've answered any of the above incorrectly—meaning that you underestimate the correct number—then you are in for a pleasant surprise as you discover just how many unknown sources there are to help you find the right publication possibilities.

In this chapter we look at how to find the right publisher for your work, how to approach the publisher, how to develop an introductory letter and resume, and the various stages of getting your work into published form.

Sources

One of the things that perplexes many individuals who have completed an article or are working on a proposal for a book-length project is where to send it. Most new writers make the mistake of assuming that the journals and magazines they read or see on the shelves and the publishing houses whose names they are familiar with are the most likely places to send their material. But this is not usually correct. Much of the time your work is ideally suited for a publisher or magazine you have never heard of. And, when you consider that there are over 65,000 magazines published regularly, that makes a lot of sources you have never heard of.

How do you find the right place to send your material? You use a publication directory; a current sourcebook of magazine or book publishing in the United States, Canada, and other countries. The following publication sourcebooks are the main ones used; they are indispensable to most writers. Just about all of them are available at your local public library. As I briefly describe each one, I point out how they can be best used. Later in the chapter, some publication possibilities are examined from the point of view of your specific profession. Also, in Appendix B you will find some specific periodicals and publishers that would be suitable for your profession or area of expertise.

Standard Periodical Directory. Lists over 66,000 periodicals published in the United States and Canada. A completely comprehensive volume, it includes general interest magazines, professional and trade journals, government and organization journals, directories, house organs, university and alumni publications, proceedings of scientific and academic societies, specialized business publications, literary, bibliographic, and library publications, and more. Periodicals can be found by categories or titles. But no information about their manuscript requirements or content orientation is provided, so it is necessary to consult a recent issue to get a general idea of what they are looking for.

This directory is best used to locate a diverse range of possible journals, from which you will narrow down and explore some further before sending out material. It would generally be unwise to send out material directly after getting the name from the *Standard Periodical Directory,* without first looking over a recent issue of the journal to get a feel for what type of material they prefer. Since most of the periodicals listed will not be found in your library, you can send for one from the publisher along with a request for the manuscript requirements. If you are sending to a small journal, say a literary magazine, address your request to the editor listed in the directory. You may even include in your letter some information about the article you are working on. Don't be suprised if you then get a letter back inviting you to submit your article for review. Be sure to enclose the amount indicated in the directory for an issue of the journal. They are not usually sent free.

Directory of Associations. There are over 35,000 professional, trade, cultural, educational, governmental, religious, recreational and other types of associations in the United States, representing a broad range of organized groups from septic tank cleaners to nuclear physicists to stamp collectors. There are undoubtedly a number of associations that mirror your interests, including professional, personal, religious, and civic. And, as with the magazines and publishers, the most likely place for your written work may be the publication of a group or an association you never heard of.

Most associations publish a newsletter, a journal, or both. These publications are identified in the *Directory of Associations,* usually along with their circulation. This makes the directory very useful in locating professional journals and specialized magazines, grouped by professional areas.

Most other associations publish at least an in-house publication. Even though the circulation might be small, it will reach a very specialized audience, one that may be quite interested in what you have to say. The *Directory of Associations* provides a comprehensive listing of associations in all the following areas:

- Trade, business, commercial organizations
- Legal, governmental, public administration and military
- Scientific, engineering and technical
- Educational organizations
- Cultural organizations
- Social welfare organizations
- Health and medical
- Public affairs organizations
- Fraternal, religious, national and ethnic organizations
- Veteran, heredity and patriotic organizations

- Hobby and avocational organizations
- Athletic and sports organizations
- Labor unions, associations and federations
- Chambers of commerce
- Greek letter and related organizations

No matter what your profession or your area in writing, there are dozens, if not hundreds, of organizations you have probably never heard of. By looking through this directory you can locate those organizations that publish material in your field.

Magazine Industry Market Place (MIMP). This comprehensive guide is the key reference tool to the magazine publishing industry in the United States and Canada. It lists every major publication and categorizes each by the type of material emphasized. It provides the name of editors and gives some information about the periodical. While it is designed primarily for people working in the magazine publishing industry, it can be a useful adjunct to the *Standard Periodical Directory*, especially in providing many specific names and titles of the individuals at these magazines. As you will see later in this chapter, it is always better to send material directly to the attention of a specific person by name instead of sending it to a magazine in general or to a nameless title at a magazine (General Editor, New York Magazine). This reference can provide you with that information.

Literary Market Place (LMP). Similar to MIMP, but it includes publishers of books, both trade and text, instead of periodical publishers. Since it includes listings by type of book published, this reference work is particularly useful for finding out all the publishers of college-level textbooks, engineering books, law books, how-to books, general nonfiction or scholarly/reference books, among others.

Magazines for Libraries. While this resource lists only about 10% of the periodicals included in the *Standard Periodical Directory* listed above, it tells enough about each listing to give the prospective author an excellent idea of whether this would be the right publication to contact. It is even possible at times, because of the discussion of the magazine, to determine without looking at a recent issue if the magazine listed would probably be right for your article. But remember, this resource lists only a fraction of the publication possibilities listed in the *Standard Periodical Directory*.

Writer's Market. Published yearly as a trade book, and widely distributed through bookstores, this thorough yet selective list of publishing companies advises the aspiring writer where to place fiction and nonfiction trade books, short stories, plays, scripts for film, TV and the theater, fillers, and magazine articles in all fields, on all levels. It is particularly helpful in describing for each publisher the kinds of submissions they prefer as well as the format they find acceptable for unsolicited articles and project proposals. Magazines are divided into consumer publications and trade/professional journals, and then further subdivided by field (Law, Education, Insurance, Optical, Retailing, etc.).

Placing Your Work

Now that you have a comprehensive library of directories at your service, the question of how you find the right publisher for what you are writing arises. Previously you might have thought there were too few publishers from which to choose. At this point, after looking over these thick directories, you might think there are too many. How do you find the right one?

If you are writing a book, the choice is somewhat easier; for there are considerably fewer book publishers around than there are publishers of magazines and journals. You would probably go directly to *Literary Market Place (LMP)*. You can then look up categories by the type of books published, until you find a selection of publishers suitable for your field. Their addresses and editors are then listed elsewhere in the directory. There is another way to go about this search, a method I use and which I believe saves a lot of time in the long run.

I might begin with *LMP* to get a broad list of publishers in a given area, say cookbooks. Even here I sometimes run into trouble since the categories listed are quite broad and more times than not don't include exactly what I am looking for. For example, recently I was developing a book on word processing – a category not listed in *LMP*. In this situation, I generally consult *Books in Print,* the most recent volume of which virtually every library stocks. This important reference work has three parts: books listed by titles, by authors, and by subjects. The latter is of interest to us. By looking under "Word Processing" as a subject heading, I find about fifty books published in that area. I see that some are trade books and some texts, some hardcovers and some paperbacks. Some are published by small publishing companies – or at least companies whose names are not generally known. A couple of them even have big lists in the area of word processing. That means that they know the market, have gotten their feet wet selling this type of book, and might be interested in a new book on word processing. I then go back to *LMP* to get the addresses of the publishers and a little information about them before sending out my material.

Two important points emerge from this discussion. First, new writers often believe that if a publisher has an existing book or two in a given area, easily determined from *Books in Print*, they are automatically not interested in another book in that area. This is true many times, but often the opposite is the case. If a publisher has done well, say with a book on word processing, he or she might want to take on another title or two to add to the list. It is almost always easier to market a group of related books rather than a single title. That is why certain publishers publish large number's of books in a single area, for example Dilithium Press or the Avery Publishing Group, the former in microcomputers and the latter in childbirth.

Second, by combining *Books in Print* and *LMP*, I can develop a profile of the kinds of publishers to whom I should send my prospectus. One source—*Books in Print*—offers a listing of all the publishers who have published in a given subject area, whereas the other—*LMP*—gives me useful information about these publishers, including their size, their main focus, location, and so on. By using the two resources in tandem, I can compile a reasonably accurate list.

If you are working on an article-length project, designed for either a trade- or professional-level periodical publication, the procedures for finding the right publisher are essentially parallel to those outlined above. Only the directories would be different. You might begin either with the *Standard Periodical Directory* or with *Writer's Market*. Next examine a recent issue of the magazine you are considering before sending anything out, since you can only really get the feeling for the type of material a magazine prefers to publish by looking it over.

It is often quite tricky to identify the most suitable magazine or journal for your article, even where a topic is relatively circumscribed by one's professional expertise. The range of journals and magazines is so great that few would exclude your profession, as long as the article is suitable.

Let us suppose a dentist is interested in the new bonding process for keeping teeth white and shiny. Of course this type of article can be directed to a professional dental audience, and that group of specialized journals would be listed in the *Standard Periodical Directory*. But let us say that this dentist wants the article to reach a more general audience. He wants thousands of non-dentists to know of this exciting new procedure. Which magazine would he look to?

The fact is that within the past few years the following general interest and mass market periodicals have all published articles on care of teeth or some other aspect of dentistry for consumers:

Good Housekeeping	*World Health*
Changing Times	*Ms*
SciQuest	*US News & World Report*
Ladies Home Journal	*Seventeen*
Prevention	

You can see that the topic itself does not necessarily limit the magazines to which it can be sent. As I mentioned in chapter 2, the approach, tone, examples, and style of the article would be the critical factor in determining the type of audience to whom it is addressed.

I sometimes suggest a technique for locating the right magazine that parallels the method described for *books*. You start with the *Readers' Guide to Periodical Literature* or, if you are using the Dialog online search procedure (see Chapter 5), *The Magazine Index,* the electronic equivalent to the *Readers' Guide.* The *Readers' Guide* is a detailed index to the contents of over 100 general interest (consumer) magazines published in the United States. It indexes articles read by tens of millions of people, and is therefore a good indication of the kind of published material that is currently reaching a large heterogeneous audience.

In either case, whether you are doing an electronic or manual search, you check for entries over the past three years under the appropriate heading—in this case, "Teeth." You may find that *Good Life* has run one article a year for the past three years on that topic, but none yet this year. So you might try to submit your article to them in the hope it will become their teeth article for the next year. You might also look through their past issues to see what kind of teeth articles they are likely to publish. As an added benefit, searching the *Reader's Guide* or *Magazine Index* will provide you with the breadth of the magazines suitable for the subject you are writing about.

What to Send

Once you have located the potential publisher(s) for your work, you are faced with the question, "What do I send out? Should I send out the magazine article, a prospectus, an entire book manuscript, a letter, reprints of my past publications, advertising brochures about my last book, my resume . . . or what?" There are simple guidelines to help you, depending on the nature of your material—periodical article, technical journal article, trade book, textbook, etc. The table on the facing page lists these guidelines.

One question that always comes up is whether or not you need an agent. Certainly, it won't hurt. Virtually all professional writers, even well-known lawyers, use a literary agent. If you are working on a book-length trade project or magazine article for a non-technical periodical, it is probably best to find an author's agent to represent you. Even if you have already initiated discussions with one or several interested editors, and are exploring the development of your proposed project, you may still want to bring in an agent to assist in the negotiations and to provide some additional expertise in the project's development.

Table 4.1

GUIDELINES OF WHAT TO SEND OUT

Publication Goal	Guideline
Article for a popular magazine	Best bet – work through an agent. Second best – send query letter to an editor first (by name!) and wait for response before sending off your article. No multiple submissions.
Technical article for specialized journal	Send complete article in appropriate form (as listed in the journal) to one journal. Never use multiple submissions.
Trade book	While you may begin to explore publication possibilities directly with editors, it is generally better to work with an agent. Send a letter to an agent first, describing your project to see if he or she might be interested in representing you. Or, if an editor is interested in your project, you may want the agent to represent you in contract negotiations. Send only to one agent at a time.
Textbook College level	Send cover letter, prospectus and your resume directly to the college editor for the field in which you are writing (i.e., College Editor, Economics). If editor is interested, he or she will ask for a sample chapter. You may send multiple submissions in college texts.
El-hi Level textbook	Query letter only. Wait for response before sending prospectus. Multiple submissions permitted.
Scholarly/ technical book	Send query letter and resume. You may want to include a reprint, especially from a prestigious journal. No multiple submissions to scholarly houses.

An agent usually handles your material for a percentage of the money earned, either 10% or 15%. Agents, however, are just as selective as publishers, especially since they earn nothing unless they can place your book. You can find a list of author's agents in *Literary Market Place*. Most agents belong either to the Society of Authors Representatives (SAR) or the Independent Literary Agents Association (ILAA), and both of these organizations have specific rules governing practices in the profession. A sample letter to an agent is found on the opposite page. Notice that some background information is necessary to help the agent understand why you are qualified for the project you are undertaking.

For textbooks, you do not need an agent. You are almost always best off by sending out a letter and resume first. This letter and resume should always be directed to a specific person at the publishing house. You may, especially in the case of textbooks, send out several inquiries at the same time – and, in fact, you should. You may also send a prospectus along with the cover letter and resume, although you may wish to wait for a response to your letter first.

I generally phone before sending anything out, either to an agent or publisher. I find that not only does a brief phone call provide me with a sense of how interested a potential publisher may be in my new project ("We are looking for just such a book right now" or "Sorry, we just signed one like that"), but it also alerts the person on the other end that your material is on the way, which will result in a little extra attention being directed toward it when it arrives.

Now let's take a look at a step-by-step process for bringing your material to the publisher's attention in the shortest amount of time. I illustrate this as I go along with some actual examples, although the names of authors, editors, agents, and others have been changed.

I had decided to write an introductory textbook in psychology. I studied and defined the market, and prepared a prospectus and outline as explained in chapter 2. My job now was to find the right publisher and to work out the best deal for my book.

I began researching which publishers had a "list" in college psychology and which books were doing well. This information was obtained by calling a few editors in the field, who gladly provided me with names of the "big" books they hoped to compete with. I also consulted with some of the sales reps who came around my office regularly.

One publishing house was eliminated right away because they currently had three best selling text books on the market and had held on to them through several revisions for almost a decade. Since all three were still doing well, I figured they would not be interested in my book or would not give it the push and encouragement it deserved. Another publisher was eliminated because it had just brought out a book that was directly competitive with the one I was developing, and I felt it would have been virtually ignored by their sales force. What I was looking for

---

Sample Letter to Agent From a Professional (Executive)

October 14, 1983

Beatrice Miller
B. MILLER LITERARY AGENCY, INC.
2775 Broadway
New York, NY 10165

Dear Ms. Miller:

I am writing as you suggested in our phone conversation this afternoon. I am an independent consultant in managerial communication, with over a dozen published articles on this subject in professional journals and in magazines such as *Forbes* and *Business Week*. I also co-authored a college-level textbook in management for John Wiley & Sons in 1972.

I am now looking for an agent to represent me in the trade book field. I am working on an exciting project and need an agent to articulate my interests and to offer me the kind of practical guidance and direction that my own experience was able to provide in periodical publication. The working title of my new book is:

*500 RESUMES, COVER LETTERS, AND HELPFUL
JOB-FINDING FACTS*

This book presents a highly effective approach to resume preparation, based on ten years of professional experience, with a unique slant (which is explained in the accompanying prospectus). Although there are presently many resume books on the market, I think you will agree after reading the prospectus that this one really has something different to offer.

I am enclosing the *500 Resumes...* prospectus and sample material. I would be delighted to discuss this project with you if you think it marketable. My resume is also enclosed.

Sincerely,

Dijon Nadusian

---

was a publishing house that had a list in psychology with some successes over the past but needed a new book for that segment of the market that my book would address.

I consulted *Books in Print* and thumbed through dozens of advertisements in *American Psychologist* and other professional journals in which new books are advertised. I asked some of my colleagues who teach the course for which my book was intended and got excellent feedback about which publishing houses did a creditable job in that area, and which might now be looking for a text. I started crossing off names from my long list of publishers and giving special attention to other names.

Keeping Track of Things

I created an activity log to keep track of my choices as I narrowed down my list and began sending out material. Before sending out a thing, however, I used the phone and called each of the publishing houses on my list. Many are very large organizations and I had to know how to find the person in the position I wanted to reach. Generally, I would ask for the psychology editor in the college division. Sometimes I was connected directly with the editor, sometimes with a secretary, in one case with the head of the entire college division.

I always jotted down the name of the person with whom I spoke, being sure to get the spelling correct. I explained what I was working on and asked if I should send a prospectus to the editor. In one instance, an editor told me she had just signed such a book and would not be interested. Another time the editor suggested that I might try writing a book on child psychology, which that house was looking to sign. By the time I was done with my phone calls, I knew where to send my letters and prospectuses. A resume went along in all cases. A sample of the letter is on page 76.

Letter Writing and Follow Up

Notice on the Activity Log the column labeled "Letter Sent" following the address column. This column records the date the letter was sent out and tells me whether I spoke directly with the editor named in the address (direct) or with someone else (*re:*). In the sample letter on page 76, I show both possibilities. In the first instance, I am sending only a letter, which is one option if I do not want to send the prospectus out right away. I may not want initially to send out the prospectus if I am simply surveying the range of publishers to see who is looking for a certain kind of book at this time. Or, if my prospectus is best sent with a sample chapter, then I don't want to bombard the editor with all this material until I determine if he or she is looking for a book of this type. In the second case, I mention in the cover letter that I spoke to Pearl Arno who has given me the go-ahead to send the prospectus and outline.

Table

INTRODUCTION TO PSYCHOLOGY
ACTIVITY LOG

	Letter sent	Prospectus sent	Chapters sent	Remarks
Mary Jane Ferrara, Psychology Editor John Wiley & Sons, Inc. 605 Third Avenue New York, NY 10016	2/21 direct	3/5		
Martin Gold, Editor College Division McGraw-Hill, Inc. 1221 Avenue of the Americas New York, NY 10020	2/20 re: Enid Cohen		4/1	
Felice J. O'Hearn, Editor, College Division St. Martin's Press 175 Fifth Avenue New York, NY 10010	2/20 direct	3/5 with phone call		
Arthur C. Green Psychology Editor Little, Brown and Co. 34 Beacon Street Boston, MA 02106	2/21 re: Pearl Arno			
Ms. Ronnie Lynch, Editor, College Division Prentice-Hall, Inc. Englewood Cliffs, NJ 07632	2/21 re: Hal Sawyer field rep		NOT INTERESTED already signed	
Toby Marshall, Jr. Psychology Editor Wm. C. Brown Co., Publishers 2460 Kerper Blvd. Dubuque, Iowa 52001	1/30 direct	1/30		2/25 Meeting Scheduled at AERA

SAMPLE LETTER

November 25, 1983

Arthur C. Green,
Psychology Editor
Little, Brown and Co.
34 Beacon Street
Boston, MA 02106

Dear Mr. Green:

I am a professional college textbook writer and a professor at Long Island University. I am now working on an *Introduction to Psychology* text, designed to compete with many of the leading texts currently used in the introductory level courses.

If you are thinking of acquiring such a book, you might want to look over the enclosed prospectus and outline, along with my resume. If you think this project might be of interest, I will be happy to send you some sample chapters for review. My resume is enclosed.

− or −

At Pearl Arno's suggestion, I am sending you the prospectus and outline for this book, along with my resume and sample chapter of the psychology book. If you think this project might be of interest, I will be happy to speak with you about them in greater detail.

Sincerely,

Gary S. Belkin, Ed.D.
Associate Professor of
Guidance and Counseling

The third, fourth and fifth columns of the activity log record the progress of my material as it travels around various publishing houses over a period of time. If my initial letter is answered affirmatively, I send out the prospectus and outline, along with sample chapters for review. Just who has what when is always indicated on my activity log. This is very important to know, not only for avoiding embarrassing duplication, but also at the point when you are delicately negotiating your best contract. You will want to know how long Publishers X and Y had your material before putting pressure on X and Y to make an offer that you can compare with Z.

The same general rules apply with trade books, too. An activity log gives you an up-to-date picture of what is happening. A sample trade book letter is shown on page 78. There are two important things to observe in the letter. First, you should clearly state your expertise as it relates to the project. Notice in this letter how I mentioned the fact that I conducted well-attended workshops on this subject and that I have a publishing track record myself. Second, if you don't speak directly on the phone with the editor to whom you are sending the letter, be sure to indicate in the letter who suggested that you send the material ("Edward Bass suggested I write to you . . ."). This reference party should also be indicated in the activity log. I have found on many occasions that even six months after an initial letter was sent, in the midst of contract negotiations, it has been helpful to get in touch with that original reference for some kind of clarification or expediting (especially when an editor leaves a publishing house in the middle of a project).

Sending Your Resume

Just as important as the cover letter, especially if you have a proven track record in the field you are writing about, is your resume. Every professional person hoping to publish should have an up-to-date resume at hand. In virtually all situations, the resume should accompany the cover letter or prospectus.

Many individuals, objective and dispassionate in their professional endeavors, experience an inordinate amount of difficulty getting their resumes in shape. There is a tendency to overidentify with the resume – to view it too much as a reflection of who you are, of what you've done. If you view your resume as a means to an end, however, with a certain objective detachment, this helps you with the painstaking task of preparation. Remember, hardly anyone enjoys preparing a resume – especially one's own.

Preparing a good resume does not necessarily require professional assistance or a great deal of expertise. It does require a certain amount of maturity, however, and a certain degree of self-confidence. It demands that you can sketch a picture of yourself that is neither too sentimental, too aggrandizing, nor too caricaturish.

GARY S. BELKIN
85 Maplewood Avenue
Maplewood, New Jersey 07040
Tel. (201) 763-2689

11 June 1982

Alicia Conklin,
Editor
John Wiley & Sons, Inc.
605 Third Avenue
New York, NY 10158

Dear Ms. Conklin:

Edward Bass suggested I write to you about a book I
am doing. Enclosed please find a brief prospectus and
some sample material for Getting Published: A Practical
Guide for Professional and Business People, Experts,
Consultants and Teachers. This book is designed to
offer practical guidance to professionals in all fields
who are interested in learning how to get their ideas
on paper and seeing them published.

I have written or edited over a dozen college level textbooks, readers, and monographs. I also serve as a
consultant for prospective authors trying to get published,
and I am presently conducting seminars for the faculty of
Hunter College on how to get their books and articles
published. During the past five years, I have conducted
several well-attended workshops for professionals--in
the academic field, in government, and in business.

Thank you for looking at this material. My resume is
also enclosed.

Sincerely,

Gary S. Belkin

You can prepare your own resume, and it might prove even more effective than one prepared professionally. But first, there are a few things you should understand about resumes in general and about constructing your resume in particular.

Studies have shown that the average resume is read – if that is the correct word – in less than five seconds! A personnel director or department manager whose classified ad ran in Sunday's paper, receives an average of 25–100 resumes a day, Tuesday through Friday – and will hardly have the time to read any thoroughly.

So you are probably asking, shouldn't there be something to catch the eye of the person reading it. Yes and no. Certainly, if a resume is received on iridescent pink paper, or with a large nude picture in the middle, it will get special attention. But it is unlikely that such attention will result in anything more than a few chuckles while being passed around the office. Since your purpose is not to entertain, but to get an interview, this would hardly be a good idea.

There is a simple test you can use to see what stands out in your resume and, consequently, to discover what the editor sees when he or she quickly thumbs through your letter, prospectus package, or other material. This test can help you format your resume most effectively, and luckily, it is a test that takes only five seconds.

Take a resume you are not familiar with and put it in front of you. A friend's will do fine. Skim it casually as it would be skimmed by a prospective employee with dozens of resumes on the desk – for about five seconds. Now, ask yourself what you remember about the resume. What stands out? The chances are that what you remember falls into one of two categories: (1) it appears in the center area, about a third of the way down the page; or (2) it is in type that is especially large or different from the rest of the page.

The resume "hot spot". There is a certain area on every resume – especially on a one-page resume – that I call the resume hot spot. This hot spot stands out above all else on a quick reading, especially on a five-second skimming. It is located about a third of the way down the page, in the center.

In preparing your resume to accompany your publication materials, you can make use of this knowledge in two ways. First, you may wish to include something especially relevant there, such as the fact that you are the president of a large corporation or that your position gives you a special expertise in what you are writing about. Or, you may wish to put "Work in Progress" in the heading, followed by the title you are now using.

Thus the reader's eye will be immediately guided to what your project is about. Examples of the use of a hot spot are found on page 81. In one example we see that the title of a work in progress, a textbook for a course in introduction to psychology, is given emphasis in the hot spot. In the second example for a trade book on the TV industry from the inside, the prospective writer's considerable practical expertise and important job title – relevant to the project – is put in the limelight.

Sample Resume for Textbook in Psychology

Gary S. Belkin
Graduate Department of Guidance
Long Island University
The Brooklyn Center
Brooklyn, NY 11201
(212) 403-1069

Education

1974	Ed.D.	Columbia University, Teachers College
1967	M.S.	Long Island University
1966	B.A.	Long Island University

Work in Progress

   AN INTRODUCTION TO PSYCHOLOGY

Professional Experience:

1970 – present   Long Island University, Department of Guidance and
                 Counseling.
                 Present Rank: Associate Professor

Sample Resume for Trade Book on TV Industry

Howard Carpenter
21907 Santa Lucia
Encino, CA 91316
(202) 344-0907

1977 to present – National Broadcasting Company

VICE PRESIDENT FOR PROGRAMMING
NBC Broadcasting

Integrating more than 10 years of experience in programming and production with a comprehensive knowledge of broadcasting, my responsibilities include:
- development of annual corporate and entertainment plans
- development of management systems for internal broadcasting and programming decisions
- departmental administration and accounting
- planning and analysis of advertising and promotion expenditures
- profitability analyses

1973 to 1976 – CBS Broadcasting Co.

ASSISTANT CONTROLLER
CBS Television Network

Responsible for accounting and analysis functions of the network including sales and market forecasting, reports and consolidations, and strategic planning.

Try and Try Again

Perhaps the single most common reason individuals hoping to publish fail in their endeavors is that they give up too easily. Over the years I have met literally hundreds of people who are fully capable of producing good to excellent publishable material, but who gave up after a few rejections. Some, after receiving a couple of printed rejection letters, gave up not only the specific writing project, but the idea of ever trying to write.

The story of how I published my first book, after several long years of frustration and several books that will forever remain unpublished, might serve as an example. An example of what? Of a principle that every writer has to understand, *intellectually and emotionally:* it is not the quality of your work – or of you – that determines whether or not your writing will be published. Rather, it is the combination of having a decent written product, an ability to search out a field of appropriate publishing possibilities, and the willingness to accept feedback and make changes. Remember, for every terrible book or article in print, there are probably several better ones that never got published.

I was working on my graduate degree at Columbia University's Teachers College, lecturing part-time at City College of The City University of New York and earning a few extra dollars as a substitute high school teacher. I was a good teacher and was beginning to make an impact on my student's points of view. From my research, reading, and personal experiences, I concluded that I had something important to offer to the teaching profession – a new method that could inspire teachers to a more sustained pitch of competent performance and offer students a depth they were not experiencing. I pursued my ideas and evolved the outline for what would become my first book, *Psychodynamic Teaching: An Outline of a Method.*

It never occured to me to ask, For whom am I writing this book? Is it a textbook for teachers-in-training? A how-to manual for the practicing teacher? A book for students or parents to better understand the educational process? What type of publishing house would be interested in this kind of book? I never seriously thought over these questions. No, I had something to say, and I sat down and said it, knowing that in time my wonderful wisdom would be fully appreciated.

Of course it wasn't. By the time the book had passed through the hands of two dozen editors, some of whom took the time to write beautiful rejection letters, I began to suffer what I now advise others to avoid: the feeling of having failed at something that was important to me. I was overcome with the painful recognition that I would die unpublished, unknown, and of course unappreciated.

At that point I made an error that in effect destroyed the book I had been working on for a year – an error I hope you will never make: I put the project aside as hopeless. What I could and should have done – and what you will do – is find out why it wasn't being accepted for publication. I can see in retrospect the situation as it was.

The 22 rejection letters I received fall into three types: 16 are standard form letters: ". . . does not fit into our publishing plans . . . Another publisher might find. . . ." I realize now that I never should have sent the manuscript to some of these publishers; that they just don't do that type of book.

Three of the letters are honest personal letters from the editor. One, from the president of a publishing company, says that he found in the book "many principles [he] could apply with [his] colleagues and employees." He went on to cite a few other positive qualities of the book, and then explained that his company had overcommitted itself to projects for the next year and didn't want to take on any others. But he suggested I send it to his friend, an editor at another house. In my activity log, remarkably, there is no indication I ever sent it to his friend at the other publishing house. I was so disorganized and disheartened that I gave up the possibility of publishing a book that had some real merit.

I then worked on two other projects, completing one – a psychoanalytic mystery novel called *Mindbender* – and beginning another, but never getting anywhere. The mystery was returned unread by half a dozen publishers and the other project never got far enough to be sent out. I had always wanted to write, was convinced my writing was good enough to get published, had plenty of ideas. So why was I failing?

Then one lucky day, a man called Rudy Shur stopped by my office at the university. Rudy was a textbook salesman for a large college textbook publishing house (he is now president of another publishing company). In addition to talking to me about the new counseling books his company was bringing out, he asked me if I was working on anything. That's where I first learned of the "acquisitions" function of people in publishing – that editors and sales representatives get credit for signing up a project that has merit.

I gave Rudy a rundown of my situation and even pulled out a few of the better rejection letters to show him. "Why don't you do a textbook in counseling?" he asked me. "After all, you know the field and you teach the course. You also seem familiar with all the major books."

"But there are so many counseling books out there already," I demurred. "Why, another?"

"Because," he answered without hestitation, "you just got finished telling me why are not satisfied with any of them. There is always room for improvement." That was certainly true. I was not satisfied, and I knew I could do a better job. "Think of what would make a better book – one that would please not only yourself but also enough other instructors to make it realistic for a publisher to invest time and money in. Then, write up a prospectus, and I'll see that it gets to the editor."

"Rudy went on to explain why my other books weren't getting published. I was amazed at how naive I had been, how easily I had given up. I thought you just write them and they get published – as if by magic. He pointed out that the first thing I should have done is to look for an existing market – say, the market for an educational psychology textbook – in which I could have then incorporated some of my original ideas.

I was determined now to begin working on a project that I believed would succeed. And it did! From that meeting came my first book,

Practical Counseling in the Schools. And from there I went on to write other books, always using the same principles of how to go about getting published.

These are the four main principles of finding a publisher that come out of my early experiences.

1. Before you write an entire book, look around for a prospective publisher on the basis of a prospectus or proposal and a sample chapter. It is always best to develop a work while under contract instead of "on spec."

2. No matter what your interests, ask yourself, "Can I take an existing form – an already recognizable type of book – and do it better. Publishers understand certain types of books and look for projects that, no matter how original, fall into already distinguishable categories. Every trade book publisher understands what a "how-to" book is, and every textbook editor knows what an introductory market is.

3. Ask for advice and follow all leads. If you receive a genuinely-felt rejection letter, perhaps you should find out what you can do to make your project saleable. If you meet a sales rep or editor, ask for advice about your project. If the president of a publishing company advises you to send your book to his friend, by all means do so.

4. Finally, the most important rule of all. *Don't give up.*

5

Making Technology Work for You: From Handwriting to Word Processing

Frank has almost completed the ground work necessary to begin writing his paper on the synthesis of a polymer. He has been working on the project in the lab for the past two years and researching in the library for the past nine months. "You can't imagine how much chemical literature there is," he tells me, apologizing for not having the first draft ready for me as promised. "I've been spending all day every Saturday in the university library and hope to begin writing up the first draft soon."

"You mean you haven't even started to write it yet?" I ask incredulously. "You know the danger of having someone publish it before you do. I thought that's what you wanted to avoid."

"I do, I do . . . but, I'm still looking up all the studies . . . trying to find out what else has been done in the field. I want to be sure to credit everyone who has done any contributory work along the way, and there's a lot of research to go through. You know in the sciences you have to check all the follow-up studies, and that's a bitch."

Liz is delighted that at last a publisher is expressing some interest in her revised project, but a bit reluctant when she thinks about all the retyping that she will have to do. She is thinking of giving the whole thing to a typist and be done with it, but the expense is high and she knows it will probably need at least two more complete retypings before a publisher accepts it. Besides, Liz knows that as she types each new draft, she is always adding to the thoughts, making changes, and doing other things that would be lost if she sent it out for typing. To her, typing it is part of the writing process. So, she sits at home night after night, pounding away on the keys, hoping that maybe this draft will be the last, or next to last.

Tom and Pamela are taking turns at the typewriter. "If we type three letters a day," Pam figures, "we'll have fifteen a week – that's taking off for weekends. That means we'll have sent out to all the publishers we want to reach within . . . oh, a month or two?" Tom is typing while they speak, but listening. "You also have to figure," he adds, "that there will be some days that at least one of us will be phoning the magazines or making our mailing lists of publishers." "Right," Pamela agrees, "and I should be retyping the last section of the prospectus over too."

Pamela answers the knock on the door as Tom continues typing, try-ing to not miss a beat. "How are the soon-to-be-famous real estate writers doing?" he hears from the foyer. A smile crosses his face. "Hi, Jack," he calls out, "be with you soon. Only two more letters to go. You've finished your work for the day?" Jack laughs heartily. "Oh, I'm done. Finished about two hours ago and went for a walk before stopping up here. But to-day was easy. I just ran off a couple of dozen letters to publishers about my new idea and completed the final chapter of the text. I didn't want to overwork today, so I figured I'd knock off early. That's what life's like when you own a word processor, you know. Zip, zip, zip. How's your house-hunting book coming along? Any responses yet?"

These three cases are typical of the kinds of practical problems en-countered by the person writing for professional publication. Frank's hours in the library, thumbing through the pages of *Chemical Abstracts*, his eyes smarting from the strain of reading that tiny type all day, are typical of the dues paid by the person assembling a literature review. Liz's conflict about retyping the manuscript herself or sending it out for typing is characteristic of many writers who, every time they make some changes to improve their work, are punished by the Sisyphean task of typing and retyping, for what seems like forever. And Tom and Pamela – well, who of us has not had to type the same letter over and over, so that each prospective publisher will receive an original, not a copy, which all the books on writing tell us (correctly) is much less likely to get noticed or to get a response.

Getting research together, having manuscripts typed, sending out correspondence and prospectuses, maintaining records of who has been sent what and when, keeping track of where key studies, data, and infor-mation can be found, editing one's early draft to improve its content and style, producing a letter-perfect manuscript that an editor will be eager to read – these are all the nuts and bolts of the writer's daily life. Whether you are a professional writer, who has this down to a system, or a professional person trying for the first time to get into print, these are the tasks with which you will invariably have to deal.

All of these situations can be handled not only adequately, but excellently, with a word processor or small microcomputer (often called a personal computer). The state-of-the-art word processor or personal computer not only helps with the typing and retyping of the manuscript, but also serves as a secretary, file clerk, and research assistant. In the pretechnological era, the typical teacher, researcher, or professional person hoping to publish would have to spend hours poring over dusty journals on library shelves, copying pages of notes by hand, and finally spend a year or two composing the manuscript. This would certainly be enough to discourage all but the most diehard writers. The opportunities for the large majority of professionals who would have hoped to see their ideas in print simply weren't available.

In the 1980s, successful writers use their time far more effectively. It is now possible to do virtually all searches of the professional literature through computer terminals. If Frank had in his office or at home a modern word processor or personal computer, within minutes he could have searched massive databanks of chemical literature across the country by phone and had typed at his terminal all the relevant research and follow-ups, including a detailed summary of each study and where the study could be found. He could even, by pressing a few keys on his keyboard, have had copies of these studies sent to him at home.

The actual writing process is just as indebted to state-of-the-art word processing and communications technology. I write all my books on a Vydec™ word processor and maintain files of current research on floppy disks that are inserted right into the machine. This type of production flow allows not only a rapid completion of a first draft, but also high speed, accurate revisions after reviews. If Liz had been using a word processor for her book, she would have been able to revise her entire manuscript and have it accurately retyped, at about twenty-five pages an hour. This would not only have saved her time and money but, more importantly, would have released her from the bondage of paying a penalty for making last-minute changes. She could have made numerous changes on the screen with each new idea she got, and at the end of the day printed out a final copy – still easily correctable if more changes occurred to her.

Word processors are used by most writers for more than just manuscript preparation and data base searching. They are integral to the effective selling of a writer's ideas. I use my word processor for getting a project off the ground, through the "ideas" stage, and to the attention of an editor – as a letter, prospectus, or sample chapter – in a professionally typed form. If Tom and Pamela had a word processor, their mass mailing about their book idea could have been typed once, merged with a list of addresses of prospective publishers, and sent to twenty, thirty, even forty publishers in a single day.

One of the prime goals of this chapter is to show the prospective author that word processors and microcomputers can now be used by almost all professional people, in all stages of preparation from writing the initial correspondence to the publisher up through indexing a completed book. Luckily, these critical writing aids, which were prohibitively expensive several years ago, are now in the economic grasp of most people who write full-time or part-time. In this chapter we will discuss how electronic technology can be used to help the writer at every step of the way, how to make an informed, cost-effective purchase decision, and how to change your whole approach to developing a project and writing it—by using technology to work for you. In order to fully understand all this, however, let's look briefly at the development of word processing.

Writing and Word Processing

The origins of word processing bring together the history of the typewriter, the development of the computer, and the fruits of a new science called ergonomics, the study of human-machine interactions. A word processor is basically an electronic typewriter and a computer combined together with a few small but critical ergonomic and modifications to allow the operator to sit for a long time and not experience too much strain. In fact, when we are making a decision about which word processor to purchase, we recapitulate its historical development when we ask the three key questions: (1) Is it a good typewriter? (2) How well does its "brain," or computer, work? and (3) Is is designed to minimize strain, increase productivity, and operate without a lot of errors—that is, is its ergonomic design good?.

The typewriter was introduced in the late 19th century. As an instrument of communication, it has a profoundly democratizing effect, giving writers a tool they never had before: the ability to present a manuscript that looked printed even before it was even accepted for publication.

Typing made the written product of the lawyer, client, famous professional or unknown amateur writer, editor, publisher, critic, carper, letter writer, poet, or common man or woman—anyone who wished to write something—uniform. As long as one had access to a typewriter, one's words and ideas could appear just as neat, professional, and impressively formal as anyone else's. We take this for granted today, when even high school students type their papers. But it has had, and continues to have a revolutionary impact on the way we think about words and the difference in the ways we treat typed versus handwritten material. It made neatness a common commodity.

With the introduction of electric typewriters in the 1950s, and the phenomenal growth of element typewriters such as the IBM Selectric in the 1960s and early 70s, typing was on the technological advance. In the

1960s, IBM also brought out a typewriter that could store the typed information on magnetic tape: the MTST (Magnetic Tape Storage Typewriter). This is generally considered the first real word processor. Like today's more advanced machines, the process consisted basically of keyboarding information into the system, having it stored, and then having it typed back on demand. But, you couldn't edit what you'd typed and you couldn't preview material until it was typed. The storage was also extremely limited.

The tape system was slow and cumbersome to use, especially for longer manuscripts. In the early 1970s the "floppy disk" was introduced. The size of a 45 rpm record, this flexible, circular piece of plastic, housed permanently in a protective jacket that is inserted into the disk drive with its spinning hub, stored information in the form of magnetic signals, like the tape systems or magnetic cards. But, like a phonograph record, in which we can play the songs in any order we wish, the signals could be retrieved from the beginning, middle, or end of the disk at will. Thus, we could get to information randomly, in any order. This came to be called random access storage.

About the same time the new disks were being introduced, another important innovation occurred: the CRT (cathode-ray tube) screen became widely available. This TV-size screen, also called a monitor, shows either green letters on a black background or reversible white/black letters and background. The CRT had already gained wide application in the computer field when it was introduced in word processing machines. The size of the screens varied, but the Vydec 1146 introduced in the early 1970s allowed an operator to see on the screen a full legal size (sixty-four line) page at a time. What this meant in practice was that an operator no longer had to sit through the slow process of printing out a long document to see what was stored. Also, by moving a single point of light – called a cursor – around the screen, the operator could get to any place on the page he or she wanted. This increased the editing capabilities enormously and made the editing processes much simpler.

All these developments would not have been of much value if the integrated circuits and silicon microprocessing chips had not become widely available and relatively inexpensive. This electronic miniaturization, which allowed a complex series of commands (software) to be stored in relatively small amounts of space, made possible machines that could display, edit, print, store, and process in various ways a wide range of documents, from two line memos to multi-page, fill-in forms and ledger sheets.

Putting these all together, we come out with what today is the typical word processing system, whether it be an all-purpose microcomputer used for word processing among other things (such as an *Apple, IBM, Victor, Commodore, Morrow Decision, Kaypro,* or *TRS*) or a "dedicated" word processor which, although it may be used for other types of applications, has been designed from the bottom up for the processing of words and documents (*Lanier, Micom, Xerox, IBM Displaywriter, Vydec, CPT, Wangwriter, or NBI*).

What Do We Mean by Word Processing?

Today, word processing is a part of a larger field called electronic information processing, which includes both word processing and data processing. This broader term refers in fact to a wide range of electronic office machines, from copiers to computers to teletypes and telephone switchboards to dictation equipment, microfilm readers and more. What all these have in common is that they store, process, or transmit information. They made do so over special lines in the office or over phone lines or inside their own containers. The output may be a printed sheet, a photocopy, some information on a video screen, or a ringing telephone. But in all these cases, some information is moved and changed.

For simplicity, we can say that word processing is concerned with *textual* material whereas data processing is concerned with data. A simple way to define textual material is that it is a string of alphanumeric characters—that is, the letters *a* to *z* and the characters 0 to 9— recognizable as units of what we can call a *printed language hierarchy.* This hierarchy (in order) consists of:

Character
Word
Line
Sentence
Paragraph
Page
Document

If you pick up a book, correspondence, or any type of written material, you can immediately recognize the elements of this hierarchy. If I say, go to the fourth word on the third line your finger can move about as quickly as I can say it. If I say, switch around the second paragraph and the third, and take out the second sentence of the first paragraph, you can follow these directions with scissors, pen, and paste. This recognition of elements is central to the editing of any written products, where we wish to change (that is, add, delete, or replace) characters, words, lines, sentences, and paragraphs.

Any machine that is to help us edit text, therefore, must be able to recognize quickly and easily these units—or at least most of them—and must allow the operator to get quickly and directly to a letter, a word, a line, a sentence, a paragraph, a page, and so on. Just how well as particular machine does this is an important determination of its value as a word processor.

There are two ways that a machine can "know" how to recognize these units and how to make the changes – that is, do the word processing. The simplest and most direct way is to construct the physical circuitry of the machine for this task and for this task only. If you build into the circuits of the machine switches that let the machine know what a word is, how a paragraph begins and ends, and what the idea of a printed page means, the machine is then said to be "hardwired" and it is called a "dedicated" word processor. Such a machine is designed to do one thing well – word processing – but it lacks versatility. That's why it is called dedicated.

The second way, and the more popular, is to give the machine a large blank memory into which series of instructions (programs) can be read off a special floppy disk. This disk – the software disk – has thousands of instructions that the memory holds on to as long as the machine is on. Until that information is loaded into the memory, however, the machine won't understand the first thing about word processing. The advantage of this approach is that we can improve our software by just changing the disk as the need arises, and that can give us improvement in our word processing. Such a machine is not dedicated, but it is extremely versatile in that it can do accounting, games, or other things in addition to word processing, depending on the kind of software we load into the memory.

In either case, we can say that a good word processing machine, whether it is a dedicated word processor or a microcomputer with word processing software, allows you to:

- type input easily with a keyboard like a typical typewriter
- get quickly to any unit of the printed language hierarchy (letter, word, line, etc.)
- make changes in a language unit (add to, delete from, or replace) with one or two keystrokes
- produce an attractive printed (typed) output of a document in either its early drafts or final stages

These are the first things to look for as you shop around and compare models, prices, and features.

Microcomputer or "dedicated" word processor? Nowadays most individuals planning to take advantage of word processing are faced at the outset with the choice between a microcomputer and a dedicated word processor. The former are sold widely through retail outlets, including department stores. Word processors, on the other hand, are sold primarily through the manufacturers' sales representatives, although reconditioned units are marketed by private brokers. Microcomputers are directed toward a consumer market as well as businesses and professionals, whereas word processing machines are sold exclusively to businesses and professionals. The person making a purchase decision will be bombarded with literature and sales pitches, and will probably find him- or herself quite confused.

Although microcomputers are increasingly being used for word processing applications, dedicated word processors still hold some advantages — especially for a person whose primary application is writing. For while the microcomputer has to serve many masters, demanding many different skills from games to graphics to graphology, the word processor has been designed — from the hardware up through the documentation — to excell at word processing and text editing applications. It is the unrivaled expert in that task.

Its screen is designed to display eighty-character-wide lines of text, featuring uppercase and lowercase letters as well as special characters, such as superscripts and underlines. Its cables and its independent parts are all factory connected and working at delivery. Its editing and printing logic requires no compromises because you inadvertantly chose one piece of equipment not used by the software designer and therefore not responsive to some of the program codes. This is a big problem with microcomputers — the writer finds the word processing software won't work properly with the printer that came with the special package and now nothing can be printed in double space.

A dedicated word processor often includes special text editing keys (such as Page End, Line Out, or Character Enter) for rapid access and editing. It also offers a degree of cursor responsiveness and speed not generally found in microcomputers. Moreover, because it is designed to be used for extensive amounts of typing, its keyboard has been especially designed for text editing applications, so that what might require many coded operations on a computer can be executed through a single keystroke on a dedicated word processor.

Still, there is no simple rule of whether to choose one over the other. It is always a trade off. With the microcomputer you get enormous versatily and expandability. With the word processor you get simplicity and efficiency.

The best idea in making your decision is to evaluate both: dedicated word processors and microcomputers. Ultimately your choice will boil down to a cost/benefit ratio. This is sometimes tricky to compute, especially where prices touted in microcomputer ads are about a fourth of what it actually costs for a viable word processor. Prices quoted for dedicated word processors are generally complete, but computer systems require the addition of several "peripherals" to get it functioning properly as a word processor. An example of the kind of advertising ploy very common in the industry is given in the table on the facing page, along with the actual cost, and the cost of the alternative, a reconditioned (or "previously owned") dedicated word processor.

You can see that the advertised cost of a microcomputer is often far

Table 5.1

TRUE COSTS OF A
WORD PROCESSING SYSTEM

Advertisement Says

Brand A Computer
with connecting cables
Regular Price: $3,098
NOW ONLY $999
25 Free Programs - Glare Free Monitor

Actual Cost

Advertised Special...$999
Two Disk Drives with controller.........................$800
Letter Quality Printer.......................................$2,000
Word Processing Software.................................$399

Total $4198

Alternative

Reconditioned
- Vydec
- Xerox
- IBM
- Lanier

word processor – complete   Approx. $4300.00

below the actual cost of a working system. You should, in fact, expect to spend between four and six thousand dollars to get a running word processing system – one that is complete and efficient, and which produces letter quality manuscript. The ads you see in the paper are often nothing more than "bait and switch" lures, designed solely to get you into the store where you can then be sold a complete system at much more than what you would have thought of spending.

The alternative to buying a new microcomputer or new word processor (which is usually over $6,000) is to purchase a reconditioned word processing system. This option is especially attractive since such units typically come with guarantees of eligibility for manufacturer's service contract (also called a "maintenance agreement"). This means the vendor is assuring you (be sure it's *in writing*) that the manufacturer of the equipment will sell you a service contract. Such assurance is basically equivalent to the guarantee on a new unit, since your service contract will cover all aspects of the unit's functioning and provide for free replacement in case of any defects.

Be sure to check the cost of servicing the equipment; it is typically between $900 and $1,500 per year. This may seem expensive, but it is absolutely necessary to protect you against sudden large maintenance expenses. If a printer has to be replaced, for example, it could cost several thousand dollars. Labor costs are typically over $60 an hour for manufacturer's technicians. Moreover, regular servicing, which is part of your maintenance agreement, can help to extend the life of your equipment to well over twenty years.

The best way to find a reconditioned unit is through the recommendation of someone who has bought a unit from a second hand dealer. You can also find advertisements in law magazines, in office management magazines, in the *Wall Street Journal,* and in the Sunday *New York Times.*

There are three things to consider when purchasing a reconditioned unit. You don't have to be an electronics equipment expert and generally you don't have to worry about being ripped off if you simply follow these rules. First and foremost, be sure the unit is either presently under service contract or that you have a written guarantee *from the manufacturer* that it qualifies for a manufacturer's service contract. This means that the machine will, for a stipulated annual fee, be protected against small and large breakdowns; that a factory-trained field engineer will repair or replace – *at the manufacturer's expense* – parts that burn out or break down, and that they will assume the costs of the necessary labor for such repairs.

A service contract, in this respect, is like a general health insurance policy: it not only takes care of unanticipated major catastrophes that are hideously expensive (a burnt-out CRT can cost $700.00 to fix), but also takes care of the small, everyday problems and maintenance that will keep the machine in a good state of repair. Moreover, a service contract generally assures *quick* response time to service calls. If your machine is down, you don't want to wait several days to have it running again. Most companies guarantee same-day responses to calls about "down" equipment. There is a caveat: Don't accept a guarantee of serviceability by the seller, since it is virtually useless. If a machine is really what it is reputed to be, the servicing arm of the manufacturer will issue a service contract warranting that it is in good condition and that they are willing to asssume the responsibility for maintaining it in that condition.

Second, if you are planning to have an operator work the machine, be sure that it is the kind of machine for which there is a supply of trained operators around. Many of the machines that appeared on the market during the early to mid- 1970s disappeared so quickly that there were never a sufficient number of people trained to operate them. If you have to train each operator yourself, you will find it terribly expensive, both in terms of time and personnel problems.

Finally, be sure that the person or firm from whom you are buying the reconditioned word processor actually owns it. Stories are legion of individuals who jumped at a chance to own their own word processor only to find out six months later that the machine they just purchased was part of an unfulfilled lease agreement and that they don't own even a slice of it. This can best be assured by asking an attorney to look over the purchase agreement and to evaluate the seller's proof of ownership claim.

Making Your Decision

As you evaluate your options, you will want to consider separately the hardware, the software, and the special features and options that can make your word processor perform jobs that will save you hours or days. In the following discussion, my evaluation of the relative importance of each category is specifically tailored for writers. The major criterion of my evaluation is the ability to generate, edit, and print short and long documents (over twenty pages). Other popular features of microcomputers, such as video graphics, budget forecasting, controlling your home thermostat, and so on, are irrelevant to writing and not given consideration here. So, if you are planning to use your computer for many different functions you will want to take that into account as you read the following.

Keyboard. It is best if the keyboard is separate from the rest of the unit. This is called a detached keyboard, and it is connected by a cable to the computer. The advantage is that it allows the operator to put the keys in the most comfortable position and it can be moved as glare and other environmental conditions change. The combination of keyboard and monitor or keyboard and central processing unit (CPU) generally lacks the flexibility of a separate keyboard. The normal typing keyboard has about fifty-three keys, but most computer and word processing keyboards have seventy to ninety, many of them cursor control and editing keys. More are not necessarily better. Some things to consider in evaluating the keyboard, in order of importance: How does the keyboard feel to the touch (don't judge at once; even a good keyboard will feel uncomfortable at first if you are used to a worse one). Does the keyboard display special characters and codes? Are editing function keys easily readable and conveniently located? Do you need a numeric pad (the number keys you find on a calculator)? This is unnecessary if you don't do much calculation and may just add weight and space to the keyboard.

Monitor. The quality of a monitor screen, sometimes called the display, is extremely important for word processing applications, where you will be staring at it for hours on end. Many monitors that are perfectly satisfactory for data processing or video games applications are unsuitable for the demands of word processing. Some things to consider are: Can the monitor generate both uppercase and lowercase characters? Can it tilt or swivel for viewer comfort? Is the monitor's color good for long-term viewing? Inputting and editing requires significantly more monitor exposure than data processing does and the operator should be able to control the screen's brightness level. Does the monitor allow enough lines to be displayed? Does it allow the full line width of the word processing capabilities? Most monitors allow 80 characters of text per line and feature 24 or more lines of viewing. Some monitors are capable of wide-screen viewing, with as many as 160 characters per line, an advantage for some word processing applications but not especially important for writing books or magazine articles.

Storage Device. There are two main kinds of magnetic storage media: tape cassettes and floppy disks.

A tape system does not work well for several reasons. Tape is very slow in getting or retrieving information. A tape always has to be played in sequence; that is, to get to the third page we have to first go through pages one and two. And, if you want to add a long block to page three, the entire tape has to be reformatted. Each time you add, the tape gets longer, making the entire process quite cumbersome—suitable only for short documents, such as letters.

For all intents and purposes, only floppy disks (also called diskettes) are suitable for word processing and writing applications. For an effective word processing system, you will need two 5¼- or 8-inch disk drives (neither one is better than the other, since what counts is how much information can be stored on a disk, not its size). The more information that can be stored on a disk, the better off you are. Information is measured in kilobytes (KB); most systems hold between 100 KB and 400 KB per disk. Since your word processing program will be on one disk, it is almost always necessary to have two disk drives: the exception is where the program is "hardwired" into the equipment – as with a dedicated word processor – and all disk space is available for storage. There you can get away with one disk drive. When you purchase a system, you should find out how many KBs of data a disk can hold. A general rule is that double-sided storage is more economical than single-sided, but in the end only the number of kilobytes really counts.

Printer. The most important question here is, How good is the print quality? Writers need to be able to generate manuscript-quality printing. There are three main kinds of printers: IBM-type element printers (the ubiquitous Selectric or "golf ball" element); "daisy wheel" printers (with flat plastic or metal print wheels having 96 spokes each with a different character); and dot matrix printers which make up their characters from small dots.

The IBM-types are outdated: they are very slow and highly prone to breakdowns. They should be avoided. The daisy wheel printers offer letter-quality print as good as any typewriter. They vary in speed from about 15 cps (characters per second) to 55 cps. The faster they print, the more expensive they are and the more prone they are to breaking down. Speed translated into output means that for an average manuscript page, double spaced, pica size type, it will take 100 seconds to print at 15 cps and 38 seconds at 40 cps. But considering the time it takes to insert the paper and line it up – both of which remain constant regardless of the printer speed – the time difference is less impressive. What does offer an increase in speed, although at considerable expense (usually over a thousand dollars), is a sheet feeder for those units that allow you to work on one document while printing another.

The dot matrix printer is an increasingly attractive alternative for writers who are considering a word processor. A matrix printer has a single print head made up of tiny pins that form a matrix. The number of pins range from 63 (7x9) to 3840 (480x8), or what are called low-density and high-density printing. Because the pins are controlled by the software, they can print in an infinite number of defined configurations that include letters and numerals of different type styles, lines and graphics, and as many special user-defined characters as are needed. The matrix printer is capable of a far greater range of material than can be provided by the 96 spokes of the print wheel. It is also much faster: generally from 80 to 200 characters per second.

The big disadvantage is the print quality. The earlier models, which produced the hazy letters we associate with low-quality matrix printing, were totally unacceptable for manuscript and letter output. But nowadays, many matrix printers use a technique called multiple-pass printing, in which the printhead passes over the line more than once, slightly misaligned each time, thus darkening and filling in the letters. Although still not fully up to the quality of daisy wheel printer output, many publishers now accept high-density, multiple-pass dot matrix printed manuscripts. This would be an important factor, considering all the other advantages of a matrix printer. Also, the purchase of a matrix printer in lieu of a daisy wheel can reduce the cost of your word processing system by over a thousand dollars. The print quality found in today's daisy and matrix printers is illustrated below.

EXAMPLE: Dot Matrix Print

```
This  is   an  example of a dot matrix printer printing justified
text   in   the   "normal"  mode.   As  you can see, although it is
quite  clear  and  legible,  the main disadvantage is that it is
not  as  attractive  as  daisy  wheel  printing.  It is, however,
suitable  for  drafts  and  for some applications.  A dot matrix
printer  is inexpensive and very fast-- this is being printed at
about 120 characters per second.
```

```
This   is   an   example  of  the  same  dot matrix printer printing
justified  text in the "enhanced" mode.  As you can see, although
it  is darker than the normal mode it is still   not as attractive
as  daisy  wheel  printing.  It is, however, suitable for certain
types  of  word  processing  applications.   A dot matrix printer
that  can  do  this is inexpensive and still fast-- this is being
printed  at  about  70  characters  per  second,  slower than the
normal mode.
```

```
This  is  an  example  of  a  daisy  wheel  printer on 10 pitch,
printing  justified  text.  You will see that it is neat and
highly  presentable,  the  quality  necessary  for  most profes-
sional  word  processing  applications.  But this kind of
printer  is  expensive--  over  two-thousand  dollars.   It  is
also  relatively  slow--  this  is  being printed at 35 charac-
ters  per  second,  or  half  the  speed  of  the enhanced dot
matrix print mode.
```

```
This  is  an  example of a daisy wheel printer on 12 pitch, printing
justified  text.  You will see that it is neat and highly presentable,
the  quality  necessary for most professional word processing appli-
cations.  But  this kind of printer is expensive-- over two-thousand
dollars.   It  is  also relatively slow-- this is being printed at 35
characters  per  second,  or half the speed of the enhanced dot matrix
print mode.
```

Documentation and support. The horror stories are so widespread that they no longer raise an eyebrow. The proud owner of the new computer gets home, unpacks it, loads the word processing software, carefully following all the instructions, types a few sentences, and when he goes to print – all he gets is nonsense. PHGSDFHOFDSHUDFSERWHOIFS!! He calls the friendly computer store and they tell him to call the software manufacturer, because there's a bug in the software. He calls the software manufacturer, and they tell him there must be an error in the printer memory circuit, that he should get in touch with the printer manufacturer. He gets in touch with the printer manufacturer and they tell him to see the dealer who sold him the wrong printer for his system. And so it goes.

I would probably rate as the single most important criterion for choosing a system the support given by the dealer and the quality of documentation: that is, the written instructions for the system and for the software. Generally, manufacturers of dedicated word processing equipment offer excellent documentation and support – and that service is built into their comparatively hefty price tag. Most dedicated word processing vendors maintain a staff of trained customer support representatives, thoroughly familiar with the equipment, whose sole job is to assist purchasers *after* the delivery of their system. Usually the answer to your problem, if you've purchased a dedicated word processor from the manufacturer, is only a phone call away.

Mail order houses, which advertise regularly in magazines such as *Personal Computing* and specialized newspapers such as *Info World*, generally give the worst support, and sometimes give none at all. Since you can't very well argue with them by mail, and long distance calls are expensive, you are basically out of luck. But this service disadvantage is reflected in the cost advantage of their very low prices, especially for software. You can save anywhere from 15% to a full 60% by purchasing your software, and in many cases your peripheral hardware, by mail or by toll-free phone. But don't expect any backup support if you have problems – and you probably will have some problems!

A reputable and knowledgeable computer store or reconditioned word processor dealer is, in the long run, your best bet. This vendor will charge for his or her service, but it is well worth it. You will get the information and support along with the equipment to help you use it. Also, the person is located where you can go back, recommend friends, or cause a ruckus if you are unsatisfied or if the configuration fails to work as promised.

Don't Overbuy

Most people considering a word processing system rely heavily on the promotions of the sales representatives. With good reason: these technically knowledgeable people, trained by the manufacturer, are proud of what their systems can do and communicate their sense of enthusiasm to the prospective purchaser. However, the questions that are most important to consider, especially for the purchaser on a budget, are, Do I need all these function? and, Are they really as useful as they are said to be?

For example, one of the most important selling features of word processors in recent years is the so-called dictionary feature. This capability, which relies on high speed processing and a large memory, enables the computer to "proofread" a document in seconds and indicate misspelled words. This sounds great, *bat at want be able two tell you that this sentiments makes know scents.* My point is that the computer will read past the preceding sentence with approval, in fact, because it doesn't understand what it is reading. Each individual word in that nonsense sentence is in the dictionary, and therefore checks out. It's ironic to consider that if this feature is used extensively and writers come to rely on it, they will stop proofreading altogether. There might ultimately be *more* typographical errors than if they were to proofread the old-fashioned way.

A specification typically promoted by the sales rep is the system's speed. Every machine is supposedly faster than the other . . . zip, zip, zip. But what the sales representative does not tell you is that the weakest link in this chain is still the printer. At the present time, unless one is willing to spend a large amount for a laser printer, virtually all daisy wheel printers impact on paper at approximately 35 to 50 characters per second. What this means is that the output speed is not increased by faster processors, for which you pay considerably more. So this touted feature is of interest chiefly to the technically-oriented.

The sales person will tell you about unattended printing and automatic feeders. These, however, are still in the process of proving themselves, and until I hear that one is working effectively (which I have not), I would not be willing to leave my word processor unattended for any length of time.

Another loudly touted feature nowadays is 16-bit processing. Many sales people will point out that one machine is more expensive than the other since it is 16-bit computer rather than a mere 8-bit. And, since 16 sounds much better than 8 – after all, it's twice as much – people are often willing to spend more.

But what does this specification about the number of bits actually mean? Technically, an 8-bit machine is one that expresses all its information in groups of eight 1s or 0s – binary digits which are the only information that a computer can understand. A 16-bit machine uses combinations of sixteen 0s and 1s. But all this goes on deep within the electronic circuitry of the machine, not outside, and does not affect the user's input or output. For very large amounts of information (such as keeping complex records on 5000 people) you might have an advantage with a

Modern Word Processing System

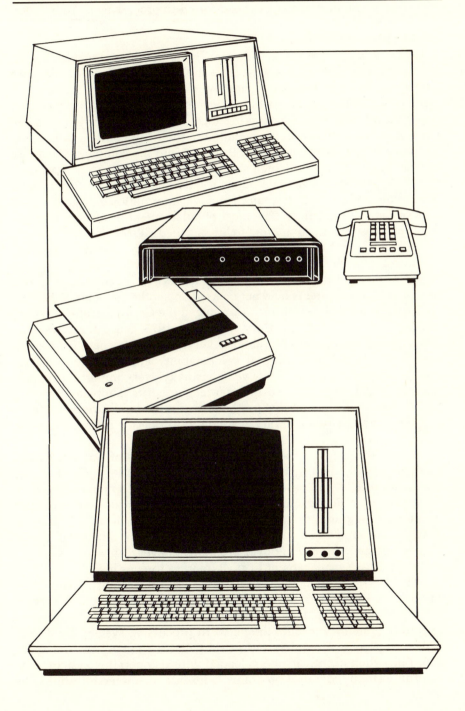

16-bit system. It is also faster for real time functions, such as tracking a satellite. But if you don't plan to keep enormous files or track satellites, then 8-bit computers are just as good for word processing as 16-bit ones.

CP/M Operating System

Because a word processing system is a complex organization of parts—including the keys, the screen, the printer, and the disk drive—that have to interact accurately in order for results to come out right, the unit requires an operating system, an internal organization that sees that all the parts are working together correctly. Although some parts of the operating system are built into the wiring of the machine, today most of the operating system is loaded into the computer's memory by way of a floppy disk, which stores the program. When the operating system is loaded into the computer, it tells the machine to print an "a" when you press the "a" key and to move information into and out of memory at the right time. The most popular operating system in small word processors and computers today is called CP/M.

When the first wave of microcomputers hit the consumer market in the mid-1970s, there was not a standardized operating system among them. Each went about its business in its own way, so that programs designed for one system could not be used on another. A small California company, Digital Research Inc., introduced the CP/M operating system, developed by its president Gary Kildall, in 1975. Since there were no competing systems, and since almost everyone would benefit from an industry standard which allowed compatability among systems, CP/M caught on quickly, and in a few years virtually every important applications software introduced to the market touted its compatability with CP/M. What this meant is that for the owner of the small computer, there was now a vast software library available as long as the system could run under the operation of CP/M.

Recognizing this, it soon occured also to makers of dedicated word processing equipment that if their units could run under CP/M, the user would be able to purchase a large number of related applications software packages. For example, a user of the Exxon 520 word processor could buy programs designed for the TRS (Radio Shack), Cromenco, Commodore, and Zenith systems—all of which can run under CP/M. This would give the Exxon buyer programs in everything from accounting to data base management to stock market forecasting.

The CP/M system is an 8-bit, disk-based operating system. This means that you have to have an 8-bit microprocessor in your word processing system and that you need a disk drive to load CP/M. Because the operating system is specific to one word processing system, the Exxon 520 word processor requires a different CP/M than does, say, the Xerox 820. But, when each machine is loaded with its operating system, they can run virtually identical programs, with little or no modification. The programs are always identified by CP/M, and they include many word processing programs.

The great advantage of CP/M compatibility is that it offers universal applications to the user. You can buy hundreds of excellent programs to run on your system. But there is a disadvantage, too. CP/M, although the first and most popular, is not necessarily the best operating system. Specifically, it has been criticized for being too difficult to learn and to use, and does not provide the kinds of protection that inexperienced users especially need, such as preventing the accidental erasure of files.

CP/M also requires an 8080, Z80, or 8085 microprocessor. These processor types are used on many popular computers, but not all. The Apple computers, which use a 6502 microprocessor, cannot run under CP/M, although Apple does make an add-on card that allows CP/M for Apple computers. Manufacturers of equipment offer other operating systems, some of which are considered better than CP/M because they either take less memory, offer the user more protection, are easier to learn, or are more efficient. Still, for many word processing users – particularly in the single-station office, where the word processor must serve many purposes – CP/M offers an enormous advantage in opening the door to many helpful software programs.

Online Searching

Consider these factual questions a writer might want to answer when writing articles.

- What is Margaret Mead's educational background? What was she doing before she became a world famous anthropologist? Where did she do her graduate work, and what was the subject of her doctoral dissertation?
- Is there any evidence linking the use of pesticides for controlling gypsy moths and increased incidence of birth defects? Have there been studies in relative safety among the pesticide choices? What are the annual sales in gallons and profits in U.S. dollars for all FDA-approved pesticides?
- What kinds of keyboards have been developed for microcomputer use? Are there any empirical studies of relative effectiveness? Is there research about the relationship of typing input speed and keyboard design?
- What are the most salient recent trends in casualty and reinsurance underwriting? What has been the general profit picture in that business? What current legislation would be considered most important to casualty insurers? What are the chances of that legislation being passed in the present congress?

The professional person writing for publication almost invariably needs key facts and specific information and data for his or her article. Often, these facts must precede the formation of the central theme of the article, and this poses a problem. In fact, I have found that a major deterrent to many professionals who want to write is the time needed for getting these facts and information. However, modern searching by computer – what is called online searching – not only simplifies the process, cutting down what used to take weeks to only minutes, but allows a far greater range of information than ever before to reach us. All you need for online searching is a computer or terminal, a modem, and a telephone. In this section we will see how it works and look at some applications.

Accessing Databases

The answers to all of the questions given at the start of this section are available somewhere. But where? We know that this kind of information is generally found somewhere in the range of printed material that fills our libraries, including

> Books – trade, text, scholarly and professional
> Popular magazines
> Professional journals
> Government publications
> Newspapers, serials, and special publications
> Reference works, catalogues, indexes, registries
> Bibliographies, encyclopedias, dictionaries
> Directories, telephone yellow pages

But finding specific information may require many visits to the library and many hours of poring over documents.

Each of the sources above may be considered a database. A database, in the way we use it with respect to online searching, may be defined as a cluster of related information about a defined area. For instance, abstracts of all the articles published about the insurance industry may be one database. *Marquis Who's Who* is a database about famous or important people. *Magazine Index* is a database that lists by subject and author all the articles in magazines. *Psychoinfo* is a database of abstracts of all the articles published in the field of psychology and its related disciplines. Each of these databases contains a large amount of related data.

Virtually all the major databases we find in the library are now available through interactive computer access. What this means is that we can use our computer as a terminal, and call up the database, communicating with it through our microcomputer or word processor keyboard. If we had to find each database separately, it would be just as

A modem such as the one illustrated hooks up your computer via the phone lines to a central online data base system, such as dialog.

Word Processing System interfacing with data base (Dialog)

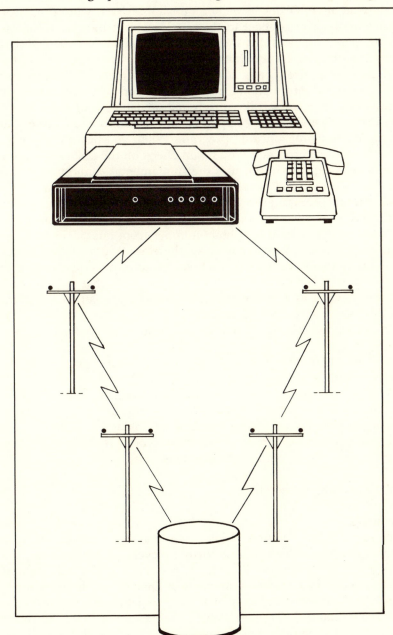

cumbersome as going to the library. Fortunately the Dialog Information Retrieval Service serves as a central provider of most major databases. You can think of Dialog as a library that contains magnetic storage information that can be linked to you over the telephone line and appear on your CRT or printout on your printer.

Hooking up to Dialog is really quite simple. Your word processor or microcomputer can connect to the outside world through a *modem* or *acoustic coupler,* devices that translate your computer's electronic signals to impulses that can travel over the phone lines. Your microcomputer or word processor also needs some special instructions about how to receive and send information through the modem. This information can make your computer act like a terminal, and link your personal computer to outside mainframe computers, and is therefore sometimes called a "terminal emulator" or "link" program. When you buy a computer, or especially a word processor, you might check on the cost of this item. It sometimes is expensive, but it is the fundamental connection between your fingertips and the ends of the world, and is therefore necessary.

The central computer for the Dialog service is in California, but fortunately you don't have to dial California every time you want to hook up. You can dial a local telephone number from one of the large electronic networking systems—currently, there are three: Telenet, Tymnet, and Uninet—that have lines throughout the country. When you become a subscriber to Dialog (and there is currently no charge to become a subscriber—you pay only for the time you use) you get a code number that allows you access to the system.

When I hook into the Dialog system, I do the following:

1. Turn on my computer and modem and load the terminal emulator software from the disk.

2. Dial the local access telephone number, wait for a response prompter, and type the terminal code (A8) and the Dialog access code (.Dialog), both from my Dialog instruction booklet.

3. Identify myself through my personal code (84939AQ), which was given to me when I became a Dialog subscriber.

Now, I am ready to search.

Searching

Once you are hooked into Dialog you have access to almost 200 databases, files of information in virtually every professional area. The strategy for searching any of these is provided in the documentation available when you become a member of Dialog, which you can do by calling their toll-free number (which you can get from 800 information). But despite small differences, most searches for a topic, an author's name, an affiliation or corporate mark, or some other key word listed in the index to a specific database. For example, let us say I am looking for information on hyperactive children. I might give the command

BEGIN 11, which means Begin File 11 (Psychinfo)
$-$or$-$
BEGIN 1, which means Begin File 1 (Education)

at which point I am placed in the psychology or education file, depending which I have chosen. I then say

SELECT HYPERACTIVE CHILDREN
$-$or$-$
SELECT HYPERACTIVE (W) CHILDREN

which means it will search for all the articles on hyperactive children. Where I use the (W) it will list articles that use the term hyperactive children in the abstract as well as in the title. It will then report how many articles it has found.

1   325   HYPERACTIVE
2   2683   CHILDREN
3   301   HYPERACTIVE (W) CHILDREN

This tells us that the file contains 325 article abstracts or references to books and doctoral dissertations filed under the descriptive term "hyperactive" or using the word "hyperactive" in the abstract or title, 2683 children, and 301 abstracts of articles, books, and dissertations that relate *both* to hyperactive and to children. These abstracts can be printed immediately on my terminal (at the rate of about $80-$120 per hour, which comes to about 35 cents per abstract), or they can be printed offline within twelve hours and mailed to me the next day for a lower fee (usually about ten cents per abstract). Or, by typing in a special request, I can order from an online vendor the entire journal article photocopied and sent to me for about $10 to $25. This is especially useful if you need an article from a journal that is not readily available. The figure below shows what a typical abstract looks like when it is either printed on line or sent by mail.

ONLINE RECORD

80008398   ID No: 80008398
The Labor Market Effects of Immigration
Johnson, George E.
Industrial and Labor Relations Review   v33n3   331-341   Apr 1980   Coden: ILREAQ   ISSN 0019-7939   Jrnl Code: ILR

(continued)

Doc Type: JOURNAL PAPER

The question concerning the problem of what to do with illegal aliens when it comes to immigration policy will apparently be around for a while. Although impossible to determine precisely how many of the persons classified as illegal immigrants are in the US, estimates are between 4-7 million. About 2-5 million of these persons are part of the labor market activity. Most of these additional laborers are working jobs at the low end of the skill distribution at very low wages by US standards. A model can be constructed and used to estimate the effect each additional immigrant has on the employment of the domestic population, on gross national product (GNP), and on the distribution of income. The model suggests that in non-recessionary times, the most significant impact of a high rate of immigration is on the wage rates of low-skilled labor rather than on the employment of low-skilled native workers. Immigration also increases the earnings of high-skilled workers and the owners of capital, however. This redistribution of income will be offset to a degree by rises in the supplies of skilled labor and capital. Tables. Equations. Graph. References.

Descriptors: Illegal; Immigration; Impacts; Labor market; Wage rates; Blue collar workers; Income redistribution; Long term

---

To give you an idea of the extent to which database searches can be used, the following shows some of the main areas of searching, highlighting the most important databases relevant to professional publication in each area. Remember that this represents only a small sample of the databases available in each area.

Science, Technology, and Medicine. The databases listed here are especially useful to professionals in the applied and theoretical sciences, all areas of engineering, medicine and dentistry, the health care fields (including hospital administration and nursing), chemical and industrial manufacturing, environmental studies, and in all aspects of technical research. They offer a source of comprehensive, up-to-date information in these rapidly changing areas.

CA Search. Contains bibliographic data, keyword phrases, and index entries for all documents covered by Chemical Abstracts Series, in addition to CAS Registry Numbers, a unique number assigned to each specific chemical compound.

Health Planning and Administration. Produced by the U.S. National Library of Medicine, this database contains references to nonclinical literature on all aspects of health care planning and facilities, health insurance, and the aspects of financial management, personnel administration, manpower planning, and licensure and accreditation that apply to the delivery of health care.

Inspec. This is the largest English-language database in the fields of physics, electrotechnology, computers, and control. This online file comprises the contents of the printed Physics Abstracts, Electrical and Electronics Abstracts, and Computer and Control Abstracts. The principal subject areas are indicated by the major headings of the classification schemes used by the included databases. Included are papers from over 2,500 journals, conference proceedings, technical reports, books, patents, and university dissertations.

Medline. Medline is produced by the U.S. National Library of Medicine, and is the key source of contemporary biomedical literature. It includes the contents of the printed indexes: *Index Medicus, Index to Dental Literature,* and *International Nursing Index.* Medline covers virtually every subject in the broad field of biomedicine, indexing articles from over 3,000 international journals published in the United States and seventy other countries. Citations to chapters or articles from selected monographs are also included.

Metadex. The Metadex database, produced by the American Society for Metals (ASM) and the Metals Society (London), provides the most comprehensive coverage of international literature on the science and practice of metallurgy. Included are the equivalents of the printed databases *Review of Metals Literature, Metals Abstracts,* and *Alloys Index.* In addition to specialized topics (including specific alloy designations, intermetallic compounds, and metallurgical systems), six basic categories of metallurgy are covered: materials, processes, properties, products, forms, and influencing factors. Coverage includes journals, conference papers, reviews, technical reports, and books.

Microcomputer Index. This index is a subject and abstract guide to magazine articles from the major microcomputer journals. Included are general articles about the microcomputer world, book reviews, software reviews, discussions of applications in various milieu, descriptions of new microcomputer products and additional subjects.

International Pharmaceutical Abstracts. IPA provides information on all phases of the development and use of drugs and on professional pharmaceutical practice. Its scope ranges from the clinical, practical, and theoretical to the economic and scientific aspects of the literature.

Food Science and Technology Abstracts. Provides access to research and new development literature in the areas related to food science and technology. Such allied disciplines as agriculture, chemistry, biochemistry, engineering, home economics, and physics are included as they are relevant to food science. Inclusion of information is geared for research by scientists, technologists, marketing personnel, teachers, and scholars working in areas related to food science and technology.

Biosis Previews. Contains citations from both *Biological Abstracts* and *Biological Abstracts/RRM* (formerly entitled Bioresearch Index), the major publications of BioSciences Information Service of Biological Abstracts. Together these publications constitute the major English language service providing comprehensive worldwide coverage of research in the life sciences. Over 9,000 journals are covered, along with symposia, reviews, preliminary reports, semipopular journals, selected institutional and government reports, research communications, and other secondary sources.

Business and Economics. All business professionals in the areas of accounting, management, marketing, forecasting, finance, and investment – and virtually every other area of commerce and trade – will find these databases indispensable. They offer information not only about theoretical advances with myriad practical implications, but contain specific data on all major companies and industries as well.

ABI/Inform. This database is designed to meet the information needs of executives and covers all phases of business management and administration. ABI/Inform stresses general decision sciences information that is applicable to many types of businesses and industries.

Management Contents. Provides current information on a variety of business- and management-related topics to aid individuals in business, consulting firms, educational institutions, government agencies or bureaus, and libraries in decision making and forecasting. Articles from over 400 American and International journals, proceedings, and transactions are fully indexed and abstracted to provide up-to-date information in the areas of accounting, decision sciences, finance, industrial relations, managerial economics, marketing, operations research, organization behavior, and public administration.

Harfax Industry Data Sources. This database contains information on bibliographic sources of financial and marketing data for sixty-five industries. The database provides both primary and secondary sources of industry data, including market research reports, investment banking studies, special issues of trade journals, economic forecasts, and numeric databases. Major industries of the United States, Canada, and western Europe are covered in the database.

Insurance Abstracts. This database covers specialized literature of life, property, and liability insurance, with comprehensive coverage of one hundred journals. Each record includes a brief abstract and is indexed with a controlled vocabulary. The database corresponds to two printed indexes: *Life Insurance Index* and *Property and Liability Index.*

PTS F&S Indexes (Funk & Scott). Contains information on both domestic and international companies, products, and industries. It includes information on corporate acquisitions and mergers, new products, technological developments, and sociopolitical factors. It summarizes analyses of companies by securities firms, contains forecasts of company sales and profits by company officers, and reports on factors influencing future sales and earnings (such as price changes, government antitrust actions, sales and licensing agreements, and joint venture agreements). In addition, the F&S Indexes provide online access to a comprehensive bibliography of more than 5,000 publications cited in Predicasts publications.

Disclosure II. This database provides extracts of reports filed with the U.S. Securities and Exchange Commission (SEC) by publicly owned companies. These reports, filed by 8,800 companies, provide the most reliable and detailed source of public financial and management information on these companies. Disclosure II includes extracts of the 10-K and 10-Q financial reports, 8-K reports of unscheduled material events of corporate changes, 20-F financial reports, proxy statements, management discussion, and registration reports for new registrants. The database provides an online source of information for marketing intelligence, corporate planning and development, portfolio analysis, accounting research, and corporate finance.

Dun's Market Identifiers. The DMI (10+) presents detailed information on more than 1,000,000 U.S. business establishments with ten or more employees. In addition, DMI contains records of all establishments in the corporate family of the 10+ firms even though these companies themselves may have fewer than ten employees. DMI contains current address, product, financial, and marketing information for each company. Both public and private companies are included as well as all types of commercial and industrial establishments and all product areas.

Electronic Yellow Pages. These come in several different directories, including *Construction Directory, Professionals Directory, Financial Services Directory, Manufacturers Directory, Services Directory, Wholesalers Directory,* and others. Each provides online yellow-page information for that type of services. A full directory listing is included for establishments in all large- and medium-size American cities. Data is taken from the most current yellow pages. Records include name and address of the company, county, telephone number, four-digit Standard Industrial Classification (SIC) code, and city size as well as relevant yellow-pages ad details.

Economics Abstracts International. Provides coverage of the world's literature on markets, industries, country-specified economic data, and research in the fields of economic science and management. This online database corresponds to portions of two printed indexes: *Economic Titles/Abstracts* and the key to *Economic Science and Managerial Science.* Approximately 1800 journals are abstracted to provide information on all areas of economics including international economics, investment climate across countries, import regulations, distribution channels, and economic structure for markets worldwide.

General Information. These combined databases provide a broad range of information about facts, people, institutions, trends, current events. Because of their expansive purview some may lack depth, but together they provide a survey so broad in outlook and inclusive in contents that they are essential, even for the technical/scholarly/professional writer. Recently, I used *Marquis' Who's Who* to check on the recent publications of a well-known psychologist I was writing about. Another time, *Magazine Index* provided a quick survey of what was published in an area I was writing an article about. The *Foundation Directory* is especially useful in applying for grant monies for work-in-progress.

Foundation Directory. Provides descriptions of over 3,500 foundations that have assets of $1 million or more, or that makes grants of $100,000 or more annually. Each foundation conforms to the general description of a "nongovernmental, nonprofit organization, with funds and programs managed by its own trustees or directors, and established to maintain or aid social, educational, charitable, religious, or other activities serving the common welfare, primarily through the making of grants." The foundations which qualify for inclusion account for nearly 90% of the assets of all foundations in the United States and 80% of all foundation giving. Grants are given primarily in the fields of education, health, welfare, sciences, international activities, and religion, in that order.

Marquis' Who's Who. This database contains detailed biographies on nearly 75,000 individuals. Top professionals in business, sports, government, the arts, entertainment, and science are included in the database. Data in the records include career history, education, creative works, publications, family background, current address, political activities, and affiliations.

Magazine Index. This database was created especially for its broad coverage of general magazines. It is ideal for librarians and others who must be able to pinpoint diverse types of information from the mundane to the scholarly to the lighthearted. Magazine Index covers 370 popular magazines and provides extensive coverage of current affairs, leisure time activities, home centered arts, sports, recreation and travel, the performing arts, business, science and technology, consumer product evaluations, and other areas.

Catfax: Directory of Mail Order Catalogs. This unusual database includes more than 4,000 records of mail order catalogs. The database enables one to locate suppliers of products ranging from boating equipment to bookbinding supplies. Each record includes the name and address of the company and such basic data as executive officers, frequency of publication, payment options, and the type of products offered.

National Newspaper Index. This comprehensive database provides front page to back page indexing of the *Christian Science Monitor, New York Times, Los Angeles Times, Washington Post* and *Wall Street Journal.* All articles, news reports, editorials, letters to the editors, obituaries, product evaluations, biographical pieces, poetry, recipes, columns, cartoons and illustrations, and reviews are included. The *National Newspaper Index* is particularly useful for answering general reference questions.

Encyclopedia of Associations. The *Encyclopedia of Associations* provides detailed information on several thousand trade associations, professional societies, labor unions, fraternal and patriotic organizations, and other types of groups consisting of voluntary members. In addition to the address, phone number and size of each organization, each record provides an abstract of the scope and purpose of the organization and lists its publications and the location and date of its annual conference.

Social Sciences, Humanities and Education. These databases are used by academicians and scholars as well as business/professional researchers interested in developing a social science documentation for their work.

ERIC. This is the complete database on education materials from the Educational Resources Information Center, which is supported by the U.S. Department of Education. It consists of two main files: *Resources in Education,* which is concerned with identifying the most significant and timely education research reports and projects: and *Current Index to Journals in Education,* an index of more than 700 periodicals of interest to every segment of the educational profession.

Psycinfo. Formerly *Psychological Abstracts,* this database covers the world's literature in psychology and related disciplines in the behavioral sciences. Over 900 periodicals and 1500 books, technical reports, and monographs are scanned each year to provide coverage of original research, reviews, discussion, theory, conference reports, panel discussions, case studies, and descriptions of appartus.

PAIS International. Public Affairs Information Service International contains references to information in all fields of social science including political science, banking, public administration, international relations, economics, law, public policy, social welfare, sociology, education and anthropology. *PAIS* provides comprehensive coverage on all issues of public policy regarding social, economic, or political problems including information on such areas as accounting; municipal, state and federal administration; consumer attitudes; multinational corporations; and Congressional hearings.

Sociological Abstracts. Covers the world's literature in sociology and related disciplines in the social and behavorial sciences. Over 1,200 journals and other serial publications are scanned to provide coverage of original research, reviews, discussions, monographic publications, conference reports, panel discussions, and case studies.

Historical Abstracts. Historical Abstracts is a reference service that abstracts and indexes the world's periodical literature in history and the related social sciences and humanities. This database covers the history of the world from 1450 to the present, excluding the U.S. and Canada, which are covered in *America: History and Life.*

America: History and Life. Same as *Historical Abstracts* above, but covering only U.S. and Canadian history.

MLA Bibliography. Provides online access to the distinguished and comprehensive bibliography of humanistic studies produced annually by the Modern Language Association. The *MLA Bibliography* indexes books and journal articles published on the modern languages, literature, and linguistics.

These databases are only a selection of those available from Dialog. You can see how answers to the factual questions introduced at the beginning of this chapter can be found relatively quickly in several of these databases. Dialog offers an in-depth, two-day, hand-on training course that is particularly helpful in developing the kinds of search strategies that can most quickly hone in on the area you want to investigate.

Increasing Your Effectiveness with Electronic Technologies

We have seen so far how the preliminary literature and research preparation, along with the writing process itself, are speeded up considerably by using electronic technology. Your computer or word processor, hooked to the telephone lines via the appropriate modem or coupler, can be used to search a database and can even request abstracts or reprints of articles. The same equipment can also increase fivefold the efficiency of input typing and then editing of the various drafts of a manuscript. In addition, there are several other areas where the new technologies can help you.

Correspondence and Mailing Lists

If you are in the process of trying to get something published, you are probably busy sending out letters, responding to editors' queries, getting together updated names and addresses of publishers, and encumbered by a lot more of what I call miscellany work. This miscellany can sometimes take almost as much time as the writing itself.

With a word processor or microcomputer you can obtain the publisher information online and store it in your system. You can also have multiple letters stored on disk – different versions of the same letter for different types of articles or book projects – and you can easily and quickly merge this information into each individually typed letter. You may also want to maintain slightly different variants of your resume or prospectus to emphasize different parts of your background or different aspects of your project, and this too can be facilitated by a microcomputer or word processor. Since I wear many different professional hats, when I send material to a publisher, I am always sensitive to the emphasis presented by the total package: the resume, letter, and prospectus.

There are two ways to have your mailing lists put in to your system. The quickest is to access through the Dialog system a database such as *Books in Print* or *Ulrich's International Periodicals Directory,* both of which provide publishers' mailing addresses. But you would be charged for this, and it is probably more expensive than typing costs. One alternative is to type addresses directly into your system. You would probably use a mailing list program that can then bring forth the address and merge it with the letter on command. To manage all this information, you would probably want – and need – a database management system, which is a program that keeps records and retrieves information that is on file.

Data Management Systems

Keeping an accurate file of who received which query letter, which sample chapter, complete article, or book prospectus, and when, is important for following up on your efforts. As you saw in the previous chapter, an activity log of the publishers and specific editors to whom a project is sent enables the writer to keep track at every stage of development, the progress of a publisher's interest, and exchanges of correspondence. This is quite an amount of data.

To keep this large amount of information and to be able to retrieve it requires a database management system. This is a program (software) that enables you to store records on your system's storage medium, typically disk or cassette. A record may consist of a number of pieces of separate but related information. Each of these chunks of data in a record is called a field. For example, for each publisher you deal with, you may want to be able to retrieve any or all of the following information for each record.

1. Name of publisher
2. Address, zip, and phone number
3. Editor or contact
4. Date first letter sent out
5. Date prospectus sent out
6. Date sample chapters sent out
7. Dates of other correspondence
8. Special Notes

Each of these eight pieces of discrete information is a field. A good database program will enable you to retrieve information by fields, selecting any criteria for any field. For example, I might want a list of all the publishers to whom I send my first letter on December 15th. This would involve fields 4 and 1. This process is called selection by criteria.

An important point to keep in mind in creating your fields is that once they are fixed, you cannot get information from *inside* a given field. For instance, in the data structure above, field 2 contains three things: the address, zip code, and phone number of a publisher. We would not be able to go into the records and obtain only the address or only the phone number since these are not separate fields. If we wanted to obtain addresses or phone numbers apart from each other at some future time we would have to make the phone numbers or addresses a separate and independent field.

Graphics and Data Analysis
Putting complex data and statistics into easy-to-understand graphic formats is one of the great advantages of the microcomputer. From your intial presentation of a project to the publisher until it becomes the final printed product, a good graphics presentation makes a positive impression and renders complex ideas and cumbersome data much easier to understand. Some examples of computer-generated graphics are shown on page 117.

Computer Generated Charts

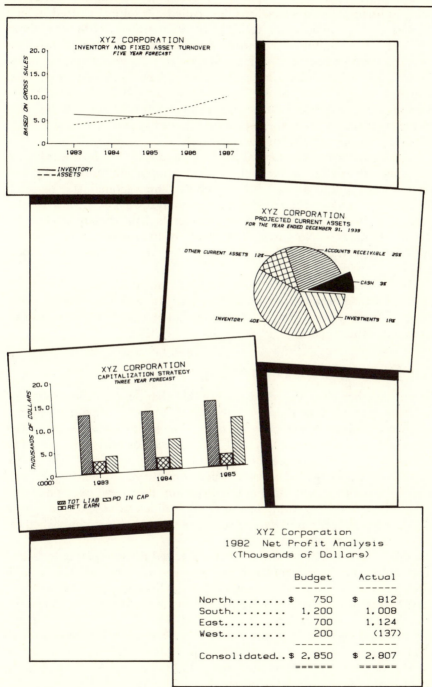

All the current microcomputers, and some of the dedicated word processors, have graphics capabilities, given the appropriate software. For graphs in color, a special printer (called a "plotter") is used, which enables each primary color to be printed separately, with or without overlays. This capability is controlled by the software, which also controls the transformation of numerical data into its visual/graphic form. Before purchasing either a color plotter or graphics software, insist on a demonstration from the dealer. In my experience, there are great variations in quality, performance, and accuracy among the existing programs. You would not want to convert all your beautifully collated data into hazy, sloppy, or inaccurate drawings.

A data analysis, or statistical package – available for most word processors as well as all microcomputers – is also important for many types of professional publications. For example, an economist, research psychologist, physical scientist, financial analyst, real estate advisor, insurance underwriter – all of these professionals depend daily on complex statistical analyses. Now, with the advent of microcomputers, much of this analysis can be done right at the terminal where the article or report is being prepared.

In several instances, I found that a professional who was relectant to write an article because of the massive data that had to be analyzed was inspired to do so when he or she found out that all this data could be analyzed rather quickly right in the home or office.

An Example of Technology in Action

To put together all of the insights from this chapter, let us look at a real example of how I used these various aspects of technology to get started on a new project, a textbook called *Introduction to Health Science.* The hardware used was a Vydec 1400 word processor with a Qume daisy wheel printer and an Apple II + computer. The software included an Apple Graphics package, a Database Management System (Selector V), and a Word Processing and Mailing List Program. I also had use of a Hayes modem and a DEC printing terminal with which to access Dialog. But any other equivalent hardware or software would have accomplished exactly the same results.

First, I learned about the market, surveyed the competing texts and read them. I made notes of their strengths and weaknesses. This kind of intellectual work cannot be improved by technology, but the next task was. Using the database manager, I constructed a file of records to keep track of my correspondence with the publishers. Each record had the eight fields I used as an illustration above (Page 117). I had twenty-two publishers on the disk with room to expand and add more information (fields) for each or all of them whenever I found it necessary. I also had a lot of room for special notes in field 8.

I then composed a letter to the publishers using my word processing program. The mail/merge program enabled each letter to have the address typed in and the envelopes typed for each publisher. I sent out the letters and updated my records to indicate which publisher was sent the letter and on what date.

The actual writing was done on my dedicated word processor. This is just an old habit since I've been using the Vydec for six years and I am comfortable with its simplicity and efficiency. I could have just as easily created the sample chapter and prospectus on the Apple II+, but the convenience of the large monitor on the word processor—it shows two complete manuscript pages at time—is not available on any microcomputer monitor.

In researching the sample chapter, which presented an overview of the major health problems in the United States today, I wanted to be sure that my references were current, that my view of the situation reflected accurately what most people in the field would see as the reality, and that I did not include any glaring errors of misrepresentations. I knew that the publisher's decision about the project would be based almost entirely on reviewers' reactions to this sample chapter, and that the reviewers would be asked the question, Are the author's research and data current and are the most important studies in the field cited? It was important that my sample chapter lead to an affirmative response.

I located citations and abstracts of all the latest research over the computer-phone connection via Dialog using predominantly the Medline database, but in two instances going to specialized databases—*Child Abuse and Neglect and Psycinfo.* Among these three, I was able to find dozens of current references, most of which led me to the copying machine at the Long Island University library, where I made copies of the articles. Thus, the searching that might have taken weeks in the past was done in one afternoon from my home and one afternoon in the library.

Because the physical presentation is important, I decided to jazz up my manuscript with some fancy graphics. Even though I didn't have a color printer, I was able to generate some eye-catching charts and graphs, printed right on the manscript. I took the tabular data about life expectancy, causes of death, suicide, and alcohol abuse and created some striking graphic material using the Graphics Software Package. This was probably the first manuscript reviewed by these reviewers to include the book's visuals right in with the first draft text, since the transformation of data into graphs is ordinarily done near the final stage of production by the publisher's art department.

As I began to receive correspondence from the publishers, I continually updated my records file, keeping track of the status of each. Some reviewers suggested certain changes in the manuscript, and I would make these changes and store the revised version on the disk. The next batch of sample chapters sent out would have these changes incorporated. In this way, the work-in-progress was always current.

The success of any project depends more on hard human work and the processes of creative and rational thought than on electronic technology, which is merely an obedient servant. In the following chapter, we will look in more detail at the human aspects of writing, see how thought and creativity coalesce in the written product.

6

Effective Strategies

Murphy's Law: Whatever can go wrong, will go wrong.
Belkin's Law: Not if I can help it.

Like any profession, writing has its own tricks, pitfalls, shortcuts, and rules. Each writer has developed his or her own ways of dealing with sluggishness in getting started, confusion over the growing mass of material that has to be synthesized, the myriad research problems that crop up along the way, and the complex organization and data flow procedures necessary to keep on top of one's material. Those whose writing is published have in addition the tasks of seeing that their efforts are circulated and brought to the attention of individuals who can appreciate them. In this chapter, I point out some things that I have found especially helpful in assuring the smooth and continuous progress of my writing endeavors, as well as the productive and realistic use of the postpublication period following release of books and articles.

There are 00 Birds in the World

Years ago, I was working on an article about the changing patterns of alcohol consumption and couldn't locate the current figures for bourbon consumption. I must have overlooked it when I was researching the data the week before. It was 8:10 in the morning, and although I had just gotten started with my work, I couldn't complete the sentence I was writing without this information. So I shut off my electric typewriter and took the bus downtown to the main library, where I knew the data could be found. A couple of blocks from the library was a shoe store that I knew was having a sale. So, while I was there I figured I might as well get a new pair of shoes.

Every time I wear those shoes I remember that long quiet morning spent getting that single piece of datum – that one fact – which I needed for my article and that fine pair of shoes, which I also needed.

A full day of writing can be disrupted a mere ten minutes into the process when a writer has to leave his or her desk and head downtown to the main library to get a piece of datum. Since so much of the writing of professional people involves specific facts and figures, finding them can prove a major time-consuming task, an unmpredictable disruption during any given day. Even using the marvels of electronic technology discussed in the preceding chapter takes time. And worse, it disrupts the writing plan, forcing you to abandon your train of thought, to stop when you least expect it. If you find that you often have to interrupt the actual writing process to get information, I have a trick that can save you a considerable amount of time.

It is a trick used by writers at magazines and newspapers, who make their living by producing copy on time. When they are working on their copy and they need a fact – for example, how many birds there are in the world – they place a double zero (00) right in the text. The copy is then sent down to the research department where all the 00s are noted and the correct information found. I have found many times that I work a full morning, producing six or eight manuscript pages with three 00s scattered throughout. If I had stopped to get the information at the point I needed it, I would have completed one page of writing and would have wasted a lot of time. Generally, I go to the main library or other research library once a week and fill in all my 00s for the week.

Using the "00" Technique in Writing Draft

If recent trends continue, the number of women in the work force will equal the number of men by 00. In the past decade alone, 00 women returned to the work force, 00 new women entered, and only 00 left. What this means in terms of population percentages is that by 00 approximately 00% of the work force will be women. This will be divided roughly as follows:

Clerical and semi-skilled	00%
Middle management	00%
Executive level	00%

Keeping Track

Many of the facts and figures you include in your manuscript will have to be documented and referenced. This means that as you write – and the various drafts may extend over a period of six months or a year – you have to keep records of the sources of quoted material, where your data was found, and where charts and figures came from.

I once completed the manuscript for a book and had carelessly left undocumented an important fact I had included, one that was central to the later argument. I had said in the manuscript, "The chances of a convict returning to prison a second time are about 80%, although the rate varies according to the type of crime for which the person was originally incarcerated." I couldn't for the life of me remember where I had gotten my data, so I spent a week searching through every reference book about recidivism and database on crime statistics that might have this information. I found lots of facts, but none that agreed anywhere with these figures. Where could I have gotten this data?

I had to take this figure out of the book, of course, since it couldn't be documented, and with its removal went a lot of the arguments on the following pages.

About six months after the book came out my uncle was talking to me about some of the subjects covered, and mentioned casually, "You know about eighty percent of the prisoners in jails end up going back to jail. Eighty percent, can you imagine." My ears popped up. "Where did you get that figure, Uncle Ned?" I asked. "I don't know, " he answered, "I think I heard it on the Merv Griffin show."

It was then I remembered that a year before when I was writing that chapter, some psychologist on a radio program had – I believe – come out with those figures and I had jotted them down on a notepad for further references. But, without checking them, they crept into the manuscript unverified, draft by draft, and by the time I got back to them, there was not way to check them.

It is important that you keep detailed records of every piece of information that goes into every draft of the book. Don't say, "I'll jot down that reference later," or "I'll make a note where I got this graph from," if that information is in front of you right now. Whether you use an electronic filing system (the database manager we discussed in the preceding chapter) or manually keep tabs on all your information, the table on page 125 shows the main categories of information you need, along with the way the information might be filed and cross-referenced.

What I have found particularly helpful is using what I call a "dual-citation" system. This is an integrated citation system, which can be used with a manuscript generated by a computerized word processing system or one prepared and typed manually. Two separate copies of each chapter are maintained. One copy, the manuscript version, is exactly as it will be sent out to the publisher, with the references as they will appear in printed form. But the other copy includes in the margin not only all the documentation notes and citations, but also, where necessary, art notes, permission notes, and further documentation. This way, all the necessary information is always at your fingertips.

Physical Presentation of Data

Many articles and books written about topics of interest to professionals involve the presentation of data. Often, data become important in supporting the key points of the written product. We mentioned in the preceding chapter how a microcomputer graphics program could be used to convert your raw data into attractive, easy-to-read formats, including graphs and tables. But even without a computer, you will probably be organizing much of your data in physical formats that include tables, figures, and graphs. In this section, we look at some general principles for the effective visual presentation of data.

A *table* is a grid-like array of alphanumeric information (letters and numbers) consisting of rows and columns. If it includes anything besides the alphanumerics and the separating lines, it is a *figure*, not a table. The purpose of a table is to show the relationship among various pieces of information and to make it easier for the reader to compare data. Its organization must be well thought out at the beginning, since a poorly arranged table causes more confusion than no table at all. A good table begins by a well thought out relationship between rows and columns. Principles of constructing a table can be found in *A Manual of Style* (University of Chicago Press) or Kate Turabian's *A Guide for Student Papers, Theses and Dissertations* (Chicago: Phoenix). Page 127 shows a table with its main parts labeled.

Figures include flowcharts, graphs, line drawings, maps, photographs, and other forms of illustrations. Figures generally consist of the art work and a "caption" or "legend" that explains the figure. Figures are never included in the manuscript itself, but submitted separately as an "art" package. However, on the manuscript page where the figure will appear, there should be direct reference to the figure, such as, "Figure 00.00 – Placement of the Figure Here."

Data, especially comparative data, can almost always be presented more impressively and clearly in visual form than in textual or tabular form. The type of visual device selected depends largely on the type of information being communicated. A flowchart, for example, is useful for showing the sequential and logical connections between events that are contingent upon each other. The sample flowchart on page 128 shows the stages of the publication process. Flowcharts are especially important where decisions are involved in producing different outcomes, such as in organizational management, behavior modification, and data processing.

Table

KEEPING TRACK OF INFORMATION

Quotations of less than 400 words	*A full bibliographic reference.* You can keep this on a filing card, for inclusion in the bibliography at the end of the book, and you might type it on a master reference list.
Quotations of more than 400 words or lines of a poem, play or song (See pages 000-000 for more information about permissions)	*Full reference, copyright holder and signed permission form.* If a single quotation is greater than 400 words, or if the sum of quotations from a single source is greater than 400 words, written permission may be needed from the copyright holder. Any portion of a poem, play, short work or song requires written permission. As you include any of these in your manuscript, note who owns the copyright. For a song, rights may be controlled by ASCAP or BMI, both of which have offices in New York and Los Angeles. You should send a permissions form (supplied by the publisher; see example in the appendix of this book), which must be approved and submitted to the publisher along with the final manuscript.
Illustrations, Figures/Graphs	Full *reference and signed permission form.* Written permission is required for "a table, diagram, or illustration (including cartoons, photographs, or maps) that you are reproducing exactly or adapting slightly. The mere redrawing of an illustration is not enough to make it an original drawing. There must be substantial additions that are themselves capable of being copyrighted. Even when there are conceptual additions, you must obtain permission to make a new version of the table or illustration that you have used as a basis for your own." (From *A Guide for Wiley Authors,* page 00.)
Facts	*Full Documentation.* These don't require permission, but you should note in the manuscript and on your reference list where each fact comes from and whether it has to be further verified. You may tentatively accept some data as facts, but they will have to undergo further scrutiny before they can be included in your article or book.

EXAMPLE: Dual Citation System

Manuscript Version for sending to publisher

      If recent trends continue, the number of women in the work force will be equal to approximately 75% the number of men by 1988 (U. S. Dept of Labor, Report #1214-83). In the past decade alone, over 1.2 million women returned to the work force, 800,000 new women entered, while less than half-a million left (Newsweek, 11/23/81). What this means in terms of population percentages is that by 1985 approximately 48% of the work force will be women. This will be roughly divided as follows (Smith and Tsuka, 1981):

CLERICAL AND SEMI-SKILLED	55%
MIDDLE MANAGEMENT	25%
EXECUTIVE LEVEL	20%

      * * * * * * * * *

Citation Version in author's file

      If recent trends continue, the number of women in the work force will be equal to approximately 75% the number of men by 1988 (U.S. Dept of Labor, Report #1214-83). In the past decade alone, over 1.2 million women returned to the work force, 800,000 new women entered, while less than half-a million left (Newsweek, 11/23/81). What this means in terms of population percentages is that by 1985 approximately 48% of the work force will be women. This will be roughly divided as follows (Smith and Tsuka, 1981):

Report filed in Office Filing Cab. Under "Labor"

  Chart from Newsweek Permission request Slip Sent 2/3/82

Copy of article in Research File

CLERICAL AND SEMI-SKILLED	55%	<=== Art: Can
MIDDLE MANAGEMENT	25%	this be rendered
EXECUTIVE LEVEL	20%	graphically?

Parts of a Table

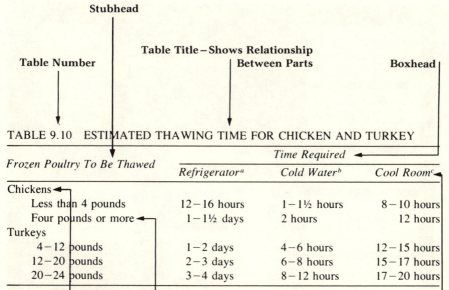

Stubhead

Table Title – Shows Relationship
Between Parts

Table Number

Boxhead

TABLE 9.10   ESTIMATED THAWING TIME FOR CHICKEN AND TURKEY

Frozen Poultry To Be Thawed	Time Required		
	Refrigerator[a]	*Cold Water*[b]	*Cool Room*[c]
Chickens			
Less than 4 pounds	12 – 16 hours	1 – 1½ hours	8 – 10 hours
Four pounds or more	1 – 1½ days	2 hours	12 hours
Turkeys			
4 – 12 pounds	1 – 2 days	4 – 6 hours	12 – 15 hours
12 – 20 pounds	2 – 3 days	6 – 8 hours	15 – 17 hours
20 – 24 pounds	3 – 4 days	8 – 12 hours	17 – 20 hours

[a] Leave in original wrapping with poultry sitting on a tray.

[b] Cover poultry, wrapped in watertight bag, with cold water. Change water frequently.

[c] Wrap bird in at least two thicknesses of heavy paper or two sacks and let thaw in a room no warmer than 21°C (70°F).

Source. Based on *Poultry in Family Meals,* Home and Garden Bulletin No. 110, U.S. Department of Agriculture, Washington D.C. rev. 1979.

Row Stub

Column Heads

Subordinate Stub

EXAMPLE: Flow Chart

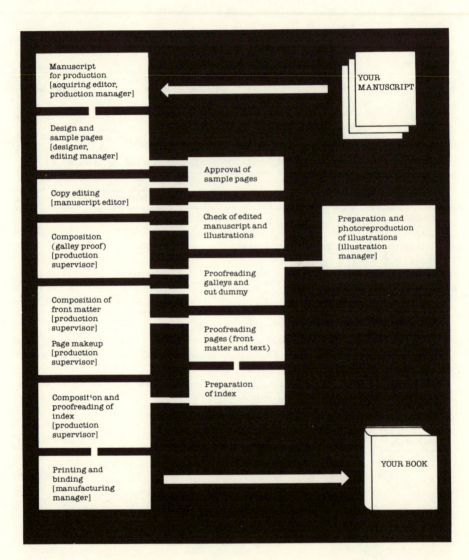

EXAMPLE: Computer Graphics

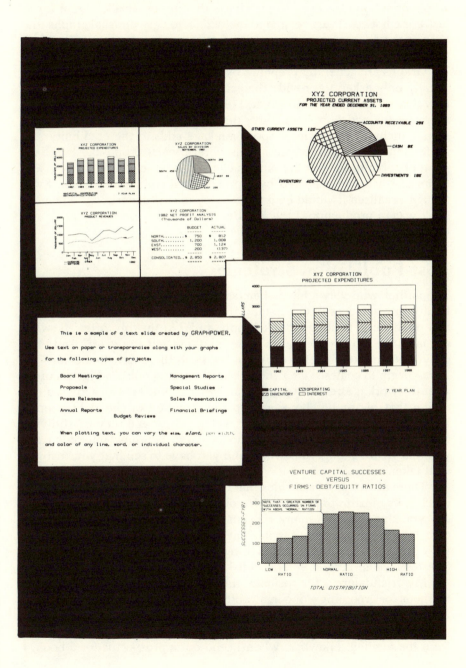

Graphs, if constructed correctly, prove the adage that a picture is worth a thousand words. Graphs comprise a variety of forms from simple histograms (bar graphs), with one or several shades of colored and whole or subdivided bars, to pie charts that are especially useful for illustrating how parts are related to the whole, to very unusual graphs that change the shape, size, or number of objects according to their value. Page 129 shows some of these types of graphs.

Graphs are generally prepared by the art department. The author is usually only asked to provide the actual data and some suggestions for how it is to be depicted. However, I have found, especially in submitting a prospectus and sample chapter, that to have attractively constructed graphs included in the manuscript package adds to the credibility and professionalism of the project. On several project proposals, I made a point of submitting with the sample chapters a large of amount of visual material I had had prepared by a professional commercial artist. Even though I realized it would be done over by the art department when the book was in production, I felt it reflected favorably on my abilities and helped me negotiate a better contract.

Post-Publication Strategies

The author who views his or her task as completed when the work is finally in print doesn't understand the realities of the world of writing and publishing. Writing a book is only a part of the job. After all, what use is all the hard work you've done if no one gets to read it? And typically, the marketing efforts for a book—if there are to be any efforts—begin to coalesce *after* the work is in production, and just as often after the work is already in print. The author should take an active role in seeing that his or her book gets to the attention of the right people. Publishers have many "offspring" to watch out for and they must divide their efforts among them, rather impersonally. You have only one baby you really care about, your work, and you have to see that your baby is well taken care of.

There are a number of rules that can help you assure that your work reaches its maximum audience. If you wrote a journal or magazine article, you should get as many reprints as you can and see that they are distributed to people who can in some way benefit from the information, who can offer you additional writing assignments, or who may be interested in some service you provide based on the reading of your article.

My friend Jerry, for instance, published an article on the proper methods for grooming a dog in a canine lovers' journal. He sent copies of his article to 300 people on a mailing list of dog lovers. He received many personal responses, and his dog-grooming institute got a few new clients from the mailing. Likewise, when I send out a prospectus for a book, I might enclose a reprint from a journal article, especially if it is relevant to the subject I am now writing about.

Book-Length Projects

With book-length projects, the author must make special efforts to see that his or her project does not die a premature post-publication death. Murphy's law is especially applicable here. The book-publishing world is rife with horror stories of books that were published after years and years of tireless effort, that were never advertised, never marketed, never sold – unceremoniously relegated to the remainder shelves in less than a year. In one famous case, author Gerard Colby Zilg worked several years on a searing expose of the DuPont family, which was published in 1974 by Prentice-Hall. While still in galleys, the book generated a lot of political heat from the powerful DuPont family and Prentice-Hall, possibly fearing a legal squabble, let the book die a quiet death. But the angry author sued the publisher, claiming that they did not market the book with a "best-faith effort" and he won the case. Prentice-Hall was ordered to pay him $25,000 plus interest.

I signed a two-book deal with an excellent publisher who had a big stake in my two books. I worked closely with them over a thirty-month period, developing books that had great sales potential. Two weeks before the books were released, the company was sold to another company, a larger one, that was bringing out two books at the same time that competed head-to-head with mine. My two, of course, were shoved aside; not even the sales representatives knew about them.

One way to help your project along is to fill out and then follow through with the "Author's Questionnaire" that is sent out by the marketing department as a book goes into production. Typically, this form will ask questions about your background and affiliations, some basic information about your book, and then some specific questions that will be important in the marketing of your book. For example, you might be asked where you book can be sent for review and in which journals it should be advertised. You will also be asked to give the names of individuals who should receive complimentary copies of your book. I recommend that you include the names of people who can adopt or publicize your book, not your Aunt Sally or Uncle Joe. Here are some of the questions, the answers to which will help the publisher understand and market your book.

1. Provide two or three sentences describing your book to provide the basis for advertising copy and brochure listings where space is limited.

2. Tell in what way this book is different from other books on the same subject. List some features not found in other books.

3. Provide an overall summary of your book on one page. Imagine

that an instructor has inquired about your book for possible adoption in his course, but isn't able to see a copy before his book order went in. Include important features, scope, purpose, degree of rigor, and unique characteristics. Or imagine that a talk show host (who *rarely* reads the book) needs the description before interviewing you; include synopsis, controversial points, and questions that the book answers.

You can even go beyond this, as some authors do, and create your own marketing manual for the book. Pages 133 to 137 provide an annotated example of how the authors of a leading marketing textbook created their own marketing package, which was distributed to the publisher's sales representatives. I have found this technique particularly useful with textbooks, where sales reps may not know how to answer the questions posed to them by prospective adopters. Note how on the front page the authors' telephone numbers stand out and the person with a question about the book is invited to call for further information.

The important point underlying all this is that when your book or article is finally in print, you have to mobilize your resources to see that it is advertised, circulated, discussed, read—that, in short, it is brought to the attention of as many people as possible. If you sit back patiently and wait for the publisher to do it, you will invariably be dissappointed.

Whereas the marketing brochure is very useful in informing sales representatives about the competitive features of a textbook, in the case of trade books this kind of information is not as helpful, since the sales person who visit the bookstores will not be looking at a range of competing titles for large adoptions, but rather will be interested in the potential of direct-to-customer bookstore sales. What is helpful is for the author to make personal visits to bookstores in the area to ask that his or her book be stocked, and to see that it is given a good position on the shelf. Speaking at religious, social, fraternal, business, and educational gatherings about the subject matter of the book and at the same time promoting it is a perfectly legitimate way to get sales moving. Many small radio stations outside the metropolitan areas are happy to have authors appear on their shows and this indisputably helps to sell a book.

MARKETING
BASIC CONCEPTS AND DECISIONS

WILLIAM M. PRIDE
Texas A&M University

O.C. FERRELL
Illinois State University

THIS SALES MATERIAL CONTAINS THE FOLLOWING INFORMATION ABOUT MARKETING: BASIC CONCEPTS AND DECISIONS BY PRIDE AND FERRELL.

1. MAJOR SELLING FEATURES AND PROOFS
2. OUTLINE OF THE ANCILLARIES
3. INFORMATION ABOUT TRIP (COMPUTER SELF INSTRUCTION PROGRAM)
4. COMPETITIVE ANALYSIS OF THREE MAJOR COMPETITORS

FOR ADDITIONAL INFORMATION

CALL COLLECT

WILLIAM M. PRIDE	713 846-4264
O.C. FERRELL	309 452-6428

Major Selling Features and Proofs

I. NUMEROUS REAL WORLD EXAMPLES

Proof: Point out the large number of examples of well-known firms, organizations, and brands in the name index (pp. 573-580). Encourage the professor to flip to some of the citations to see how the examples are employed. Take a copy of the book and underline the names of companies, organizations, and brands in several of the chapters. When flipping through the book to show examples, focus on chapters 6 through 13 (pages 153 to 388) and chapters 18 to 20 (pages 501 to 572) because these chapters have the greatest concentration of examples.

II. READABILITY

Proof: The writing is straightforward and is not complex. The reading level is designed to communicate with college sophomores and juniors. The reading level is not so low as to be insulting. Yet, not so high as to be over their heads. Most of the students who use the book like the reading level. To provide more proof, you might encourage the professor to have several of his or her students read several chapters to evaluate the book's readability.

III. COMPREHENSIVENESS OF COVERAGE

Proof: The table of contents is reasonably well detailed. Use it to demonstrate the vast array of topics that are covered. If the professor is interested in a specific topic, go immediately to the index.

IV. DEPTH OF COVERAGE

Proof: Our text provides greater depth of coverage on most topics than does our competition. To demonstrate depth of coverage, use chapter 13 and chapter 15, both of which are especially detailed.

V. LARGE NUMBER OF WELL-DEVELOPED ANCILLARIES

Proof: Enumerate the list of ancillaries that are available. When the potential adopter shows an interest in any particular one, give him or her more details. More details on the ancillaries are shown on the following pages.

Description of the Ancillaries

A. Instructor's Manual

    1. Very complete
    2. Contents
       a. Purpose and perspective-- conversation
         with the teacher
       b. Lecture outlines-- competitors do not have these. They are
         very thorough, allowing the teacher to lecure directly from
         the manual. Good especially for new teachers and teaching
         assistants.
       c. Involvement exercises: Create situations that allow students
         to "experience" various aspects of marketing. Sometimes
         these are called experiental exercises.
       d. Transparancies-- print is large

B. Test Bank I

    1. Approximately 50 MC and 50 TF for each chapter, over 200
       questions
    2. Most of the MC have five alternatives
    3. Perforated format. Benefits: eliminates tying, proofreading,
       and student frustration over errors
    4. Computer-assisted Test Program

C. Test Bank II

    1. Provides approximately 25 additional multiple choice questions
      beyond those in Test Bank I
    2. Questions are more applications-oriented than those in Test Bank I

D. Readings Book

    1. Contains 50 articles
    2. Purposes:
       a. To expand upon and amplify some topics mentioned in the main
         test
       b. To show the application of marketing decisions and ac-
         tivities
       c. To make marketing more lively in the classroom

E. Study Guide

    1. More complete than any competitor's
    2. Designed for self-study
    3. Contents
       a. Chapter summary
       b. True-false statements (20-25)
       c. Multiple choice questions (20-25)
       d. Programmed completion exercises

COMPETITIVE ANALYSIS OF

Bergin's <u>INTRODUCTION TO MARKETING</u> (Fourth Edition)

Published by Taylor-Hall

(This book competes with the Pride/Ferrel basic marketing package)

The primary focus of this competitive analysis is to discuss the major differences between this new edition and the previous (third) edition. Because there are relatively few differences between the editions, major excerpts from the competitve analysis of the third edition are also presented because much of it is quite applicable to the new edition.

COMPARISON OF THE NEW AND PREVIOUS EDITIONS

As reflected above, the most outstanding chacteristic of the latest edition is that it is so strikingly similar to the previous edition in terms of content, artwork, and layout. The new edition is thinner but is actually 73 pages longer than the old edition. The new edition has two less chapters. This was achieved by replacing one chapter with an appendix (after the third chapter) and by combining two chapters into one. Thus, the new edition containsthe same material as the previous edition.

Although the new edition is as comprehensive as the old one, it is also just as dull and boring. Bergin has made an unsuccessful attempt to liven up his book by adding a considerable amount of photography. These photographs have simply been dropped in to help break up page after page of descriptive material. It is obvious that the photographs have been put in strictly for cosmetic purposes because he never refers to them in the text material. In fact, there are no figure numbers on them for reference purposes.

The new edition contains 30 short cases located at the end of the book. Most of these cases appear to be new ones. Yet, they are not about real companies. All of the cases are apparently hypothetical thus making them less interesting.

The supplementary components for this book are the same except the publisher has added a computerizedtest bank. This is a component that we pioneered in the basic marketing textbook market.

EXCERPTS FROM THE COMPETITVE ANALYSIS OF TH PREVIOUS EDITION.

About 25% of the market is using this text. One of the major weaknesses is that it does not use real-world examples as extensively as we do. The book does not cover the environmental variables adequately, and nonbusiness marketing is not covered. In addition, Bergin's definition is becoming outdated as the exchange notion of marketing becomes more popular. The end-of-chapter materials are highly limited.

COMPETIVE INFORMATION

Bieber's Foundations of Marketing, 5th Edition, Wm. C. Brown,
        1983, 609 pp. (Competes with Pride/Ferrell)

The new edition of Bieber is shorter, is lower level, and has been
redesigned to compete head-on with Caner/Smith. A high school level
art design with in-house cartoons to illustrate marketing concepts
appears to be aimed at the JC and CC level adopter.

Depth of Coverage -- Much content has been removed from the 1978
edition to make the text shorter. Pride/Ferrell offers more depth and
breadth in coverage of important marketing mix areas. For example,
look at Bieber's Chapter 12 (Management of Advertising). Pride/Ferrell's
coverage is much more comprehensive and covers topics in depth.
Bieber even points out the superfciality of coverage by the following
statement in his preface: "this edition is about 20 percent shorter
than the previous one, primarily a reduction of the depth of detail in
many sections."

Illustrations -- The art program is a major weakness of the new
edition. Most potential adopters should object to the way marketing is illustrated in high school level drawings. The art design
ruins the impact of some text material by confusing the student with
meaningless or misleading artwork. Ask the professor to look at
Stanton's cartoon illustration of "demand is inelastic" on page 151.
Also, the cartoon illustration of market differentiation on page 201
and the priced line cartoon on page 285 do not illustrate the intended concepts. Ask the professor if the illustration on page 50
contributes to the understanding of the types of data sources. These
cartoons only get in the way of a clear understanding of the text
material. Pride/Ferrell uses better illustrations to clearly inform
the student.

Basic Approach -- Bieber still uses a systems framework. Our surveys
indicate that professors do not like to use the systems approach in
basic marketing. Bieber's Chapter 4 is entitled "Marketing Systems
and the Marketing Environment". His first topic in this chapter is
the "Systems Apprach to Marketing".

Advantages of Pride/Ferrell Over Bieber

Pride/Ferrell has:

1. Greater depth of coverage
2. An effective art program that clearly illustrates and exemplifies
   concepts. Our artwork communicates with students rather than
   insults them.
3. Greater readability
4. Almost twice as many cases
5. More ancillary materials
6. More real-world examples

7

Advice from Writers and Editors

This chapter presents a view of the five most common areas of concern to writers and editors alike, put together from my informal interviews with a half-dozen editors and nine writers about how best to overcome many of the thorny problems all authors face. Names of books and publishing houses have been changed, along with some alterations of detail to conceal identities. Otherwise, all the information is factual.

Negotiating a Contract

What should an author look for in a book contract?

Most inexperienced writers look at only two things in a contract – the advance and the royalty percentage. Ask just about any new writer which is better, a contract with a $3,000 advance and a 12% royalty or a contract with a $10,000 advance and a 15% royalty, and they will all choose the latter. All of them. Yet, the advance and the royalty percentage are two small parts of the total contract. There are major differences between a textbook contract and a trade book contract, but in both cases some familiarity with the major points of negotiation can make a substantial difference in the actual profits realized from a project.

Two general things to recognize about royalties. A royalty is defined as a percentage of the publisher's income that is directed to an author. But how is the income base determined? Generally, a distinction is made between the gross and net receipts. A royalty contract may specify 15% of gross receipts or 15% of net receipts. Consider what this difference means for a book that retails for $20.00. At fifteen percent of the *gross,* the royalty amounts to $3.00 per copy. If the royalty is based on *net* receipts, however, then the author of a twenty-dollar textbook (discounted to the bookstore at 20%) would receive $2.40 per copy (15% of $16.00) while the author of a twenty-dollar trade book would receive $1.80 per copy (15% of $12.00)

Terms for royalty percentage may also vary according to the type of sale or the total number of copies sold. Large sales (to book clubs, corporations, college course adoptions) generally yield a lower royalty percentage. Sales to foreign book distributors also yield a partial royalty. Some royalty schedules increase the percentage after a certain number of copies have been sold—often the number of copies the publisher feels is necessary to pay back the initial investment. This is called a *sliding scale* royalty. All these factors should be carefully weighed in negotiating a contract or in evaluating your potential income from a proposed writing project.

An Editor Speaks about Contracts

Our publishing house had two big-name authors whom we desperately wanted to sign to do a biology text. We figured we could sell 25,000 copies the first year with their names and reputations, but they wanted a gigantic advance—I think about $60,000. Well, we worked out a deal where they would get that advance, but a smaller royalty, 12% instead of 15%, with no sliding to 18% above 25,000 copies for this edition as we did with others. They also agreed to pay for all the art, including preparation, permissions, and to have the ancillaries (student workbook, test questions, and an instructor's manual) prepared. They saw that a long way down the road, and they needed the money now.

At about the same time, I signed a young woman from a community college to do a nursing text. We figured the sales potential in the 10-20,000 range. Her husband was in publishing and worked out the following deal for her: she would receive a $1,000 advance, because he knew we weren't eager to lay out much at the beginning for an unknown entity like her. But, in return for this acquiescence, she was given a grant of $1,000. (The difference between "advance" and "grant" is that advance money is charged against eventual royalties, while grant money—which is theoretically used for manuscript preparation and to defer preparation costs—is not charged against your royalty account; that is, it is profit *above* your royalties). Her royalty was sliding-scale: 12%, 15%, 18%, the latter, quite frankly, for sales we did not believe the book would ever achieve. Also, she crossed off the paragraphs that required her to do the ancillaries, so we agreed to foot the bill for the instructors' manual and workbook, which we had prepared in-house, as it turned out. We did this partly in return for our low investment in the project. We wanted to free up as much capital as possible. She was required to pay for half the art permissions (fees for using photographs, figures, and numeric graphs from other sources) and all of the textual permissions (quotations above a certain number of words from copyrighted sources).

Both books, as it turned out, sold about the same number of copies in the four years of their first edition. This is what their payout looked like.

Biology		Nursing	
41,000 $1.43 @ each	$58,630	15,000 @ $1.43 (12%) each	$21,450
Art Fees	$ 4,618	10,000 @ $1.61 (15%) each	$16,100
Permissions	$ 1,090	16,000 @ $1.80 (18%) each	$28,800
Art Prep	$ 2,986	Grant	$ 1,000
Instructors' Manual Prep	$ 1,000	Permissions	$ 1,150
Student Workbook Prep	$ 1,150	Half of Art Fee	$ 2,300
Index	$ 700		
Total	$47,086	Total	$63,900

As you can see, in the long run the biology writers never earned enough to repay their advance. The nursing writer did a lot better, even though her advance was paltry compared with the big guns in biology.

Response from a Writer
From my experiences, the example cited above is hardly typical. I always try for the largest advance I can get, and am especially eager to sign for grant money, since it is money above what I will receive in royalties.

I have found that the larger the advance, the more effort and push the publisher puts behind the book. Even in the case above, you can bet your boots that the publisher had a lot more riding on the book with the $60,000 advance than the book with the $1,000 advance. So when the sales reps were given their hype, when the advertising budget was decided, and when the allocation of resouces was divided among the list, I'm sure the high advance book was given priority over the other. Why they ultimately achieved equal sales – that's a different question.

But the main point is that a big advance just about guarantees that the publisher will work its butt off to get its money back. And it means that you as the author have that money interest-free between writing the book and when the royalties are earned. Of course, too much of a trade-off, which may be what those authors got, is not a good idea, either. But I would have gone along with them and gone for the big advance.

Some Recommendations
The best advice in negotiating a contract is to look at each part in relation to the whole. If you just look at a contract as a group of independent clauses, each unrelated to the other, you miss the point of its function as an integrated document. And yet, as attorney and contract specialist Richard Hofflich points out, "This view of the contract as a whole has its

pitfalls. A document that flows from one clause into another provides a natural camouflage for concealing material phrases. The "simple" contract can, and often does, kindle the spark of litigation. One should read the entire agreement only for overview, then dissect the paragraphs word by word." And, I might add, one should have a lawyer or agent look it over before signing.

To appreciate some of the problems, let's look at the main negotiable clauses in the contract to see how the total generally adds up to the sum of negotiable parts. These clauses are taken from the standard textbook contract issued by most publishers. Since the contracts are drawn by the publisher, we should expect that the language and terms reflects to the publisher's advantage, and this is generally the case. In each of the following clauses, I have put in bold letters some of the hidden dangers to the author.

Royalty Clause in a Textbook Contract

The Publisher agrees to pay the author a royalty on books sold by the Publisher according to the following schedule:
   Domestic Royalty: **15%** of the actual monies received by the publisher for all copies sold.
   Foreign and **Non-College Adoption Sales** – One-half the domestic rate.

The above probably looks innocuous enough. But consider these three things. "Foreign" sales includes sales in Canada, which may represent a sizable percentage of the total sales. One of my own textbooks has sold more copies in Canada than in the United States, yet I receive only half as much royalty on it. There may be nothing you can do about this if the publisher is represented in Canada by a book distributing agent that earns the half of the royalty as its fee, but you should at least explore whether Canada can be excluded from the foreign sales royalty rate.

A more serious flaw, perhaps, is the half-royalty for "non-college adoption sales." If, by some stroke of luck, your book became a runaway bestseller and sold a million copies, you would get only half your royalty for each copy because these sales are not part of an adoption. Also, you should keep in mind that small sales can often add up to large orders during a single royalty period (six months). And notice, too, that as written it states "non-college" adoption sales. Technically, this would include sales to the military. So try to avoid having such a phrase in your royalty clause or clarify its meaning before signing.

Finally, I advise my clients to negotiate a sliding scale of royalty payments, with the author's percentage increasing, usually from 10% to 15% or from 15% to 18-3/4% as sales rise. Most publishers are willing to go along with this, since they are first and foremost interested in recouping their costs and then willing to share the profits with the author. Once you figure out how many copies the publisher has to sell to break even, you can usually arrange for an higher royalty above that number of copies.

Improved Royalty Clause in a Textbook Contract

> The Publisher agrees to pay the author a royalty on all copies of said work sold by the Publisher and paid for, as follows:
> On all adoption orders originating in the United States and Canada, fifteen percent (15%) of the actual invoice value of the first 5,000 of such copies sold, and eighteen and three-quarters percent (18-3/4%) of the actual invoice value on all copies over 5,000. "Adoption orders" are defined to be orders for the said work of ten copies or more.
> On all other sales, twelve percent (12%) of the actual invoice value.

Trade book contracts pose more complex problems, both in terms of royalty arrangements and what are called subsidiary rights—including paperback reprint rights, movie rights, serial and book club rights, etc. These rights often add up to much more than the royalty earned by the hardcover book. The Author's Guild, a non profit professional organization of writers, has available for its members a model trade book contract that should be consulted before signing the publisher's standard contract. The model contract is available from the Author's Guild at 234 West 44th Street, New York, NY 10036. They recommend a very detailed clause to protect the author on the matter of royalty.

The next two clauses are often skimmed when scrutinizing the terms of a contract, but both could prove very costly. They are tucked in there innocuously enough, but watch out. They have important implications that can cost you not only money, but time as well.

Keys, Manuals, and Ancillary Materials Clause in a Textbook Contract

The author will prepare for the Publisher any teachers' manuals, keys, answer books, or such materials which the Publisher decides are necessary for the successful marketing of the Work, including a test bank. When requested by the Publisher, in order to promote the sale of the Work, the Author will assist the Publisher in the planning of suitable teaching pictures, diagrams, charts, photographs, maps, and other graphic aids that may be needed to illustrate or to increase the teaching effectiveness of the Work, and will provide the Publisher with specifications and pencil sketches for art work and diagrams that may be required. No royalty will be paid on such auxiliary materials. If for any cause the Author does not prepare these auxiliary materials within six months of a written request from the Publisher that he do so, the Author agrees that the materials may be prepared by a competent person or persons selected by the Publisher and that the cost thereof shall be charged to the Author's royalty account.

Permissions Clause in a Textbook Contract

The author hereby agrees to assume all expenses which he may incur in obtaining permissions to include in said Work copyrighted textual and art material controlled by others. The Publisher agrees to make payment for such permission fees on the date of publication, said payment not to exceed six thousand dollars, and to be debited against the author's general royalty account on the first monies earned.

The first clause says that the author is required to prepare the auxiliary material (sometimes called "supplementary materials" or "ancillaries") requested by the publisher, for which he or she will not be paid. This material is generally provided free to instructors who adopt the book or are considering adoption. But since the cost of its physical production is usually less than the hours and expenses needed for its preparation, the author in effect underwrites a large percentage of its preparation expenses.

I have found, in fact, that the preparation of these materials can sometimes take almost as long as writing the book did – and can prove far more aggravating. For one project, I had to prepare and field-test 1,500 multiple-choice test questions and 200 essay questions, which then had to be revised and rewritten in light of the field testing. This was extremely time consuming and difficult, but if I had not personally undertaken the project I would have been required to underwrite the cost from my royalties. Especially now, when publishers are looking at microcomputers as teaching aids, there are many auxiliaries that authors are asked to prepare.

An instructor's kit may include a manual that can run several hundred pages, usually with teaching suggestions, resources for the classroom (including films, tapes and overhead transparencies), a more detailed elaboration of the material in the text, discussion questions, suggested readings, annotated bibliographies, and more. In some markets, such as educational psychology and marketing, the quality and content of the instructor's manual is important in helping the sale of the book, so publishers spend a great deal of time on its development. But, since the author is responsible for the creation, he or she does the work under the publisher's supervision and does not receive any direct remuneration.

I generally argue as determinedly as possible to negotiate myself free of these responsibilities since I'm do to get a bigger advance or a higher royalty. I am not always successful, but many times the editor realizes that I would do best – both for myself and the publishing house – concentrating all my energy on the manuscript. I have found that my exemption from these responsibilities not only saves me a good six to nine months of tedious work, but that when the task of developing ancillaries is entrusted to the hands of professionals who are totally concerned with their development, a better product is invariably the result.

Improved Ancillaries Clause in a Textbook Contract

The Author agrees to advise the Publisher and act as the final reviewer on any teacher's manuals, keys, answer books, or such material which the Publisher, at the Publisher's expense, prepares for the Work.

The permissions clause may prove to be a small problem or a large problem depending on the nature of the book. If you are preparing a reader, textual permissions can add up to thousands of dollars. Rarely will a publisher be willing to absorb these costs unless you take a significant cut on your royalty percentage. With a large introductory textbook, the art permissions can be quite expensive. A book with fifty line drawing and 100 photos can run about $6,000 in permissions fees.

When many authors negotiate a contract, they look only at the "up front" money, and forget about the costs that will be charged against their royalty accounts when the book begins to sell. The temptation of getting a $5,000 advance far outweighs the reasonable analysis of what costs you will incur as the project develops. Yet these expenses can be quite high. I suggest you attempt to have the publisher absorb the costs, or at least half the costs, of the art and textual permissions fees. They are sometimes willing to do this to sign a book they want very badly, or sometimes they do it in exchange for a smaller advance.

Improved Permission Clause in a Textbook Contract

> The Author will furnish rough sketches to the Publisher, and the Publisher will prepare for publication at the Publisher's expense, up to 25 drawings and graphs. The Publisher agrees to pay for the cost of providing up to a maximum of 50 acceptable photographs for illustrating text material at a cost not to exceed $3,000. The cost of such photographs shall include the right to copyright and their use for any purpose, including textbook illustrations, advertising, display, exhibitions, art purposes, and trade, without any restrictions, reservations, or limitations whatsoever.

In negotiating a trade book contract, as I mentioned earlier, the problems are more complex. Publishing practices, as well as marketing and distribution options, leave room for many areas of negotiation that are not common to the text book field. Consider the book club, paperback, and secondary rights for example. These are irrelevant in textbook contracts, but require a lengthy clause, such as that below, for a trade book. In addition to this, other contract clauses have to account for first serial rights, for stage, phonograph, radio, motion picture, television, computer, microfilm, and other audio-visual rights, as well as for foreign rights. For this reason, I suggest an agent or attorney help you evaluate your contract, or that you consult the Author's Guild contract as a model.

In addition to these clauses, the main negotiable points with which you will be concerned as you negotiate your contract are the advance, grant, and royalty amounts. There are no fixed rules here, but generally publishers are reluctant to provide any sizable grants, since the cost of a grant must then be built into the book's production costs (that is, grant money is not reimbursable to the publisher as advance money is, since the advance is later debited from the author's royalty account). There is no firm rule for negotiating an advance, but my informal survey shows the typical advance for a college textbook nowadays is between $4,000 and $25,000. Many of the larger advances of yesteryear proved disastrous, when books were not delivered or did not sell as expected. The amount a publisher will be willing to advance depends in the end on the size of the potential market, the author's previous track record, and the publisher's enthusiasm for the book.

Predictable Problems

What have you consistently found to be the most common problems authors and editors face in the development of a book?

Several areas of problems were repeatedly mentioned, but probably the most troublesome one for editors is manuscripts coming in late. Editors would typically say that although they really didn't expect first drafts to be submitted on time, they at least hoped that the final manuscript would be in the publisher's office within six months of deadline; but delays sometimes go to a year or more. In textbook publishing, where the publication date of a book can mean the gain or loss of a term's adoption, this is especially troublesome. I heard several stories of major market books that had to make their bow in the midst of formidable competition the publisher was hoping to avoid, only because the author's dilatoriness forced the publication date to be moved up a full year.

Authors admitted that they had been dilatory in meeting some of their due date obligations, but suggested that some causes of publishing delay may be attributable to the publishers, editors, or reviewers as well. "I had my first draft in around the middle of July," one author told me, "and expected to have the reviews back and a final draft in by mid-November. But I couldn't move along until I had all the reviews in. My editor told me we needed five reviews. Well, two came back pretty soon, but months went by before the others were in, and I couldn't be expected to begin the rewriting before I knew what the other reviewers were going to say. So I didn't even begin writing the final draft before late October."

Authors also complained about their editors leaving the publishing house and their book getting lost somewhere in the middle. "I had an editor who was very enthusiastic about my book," one author explained. "She was working with me all along on its development, and we agreed we would be trying out a unique approach. But she left pretty suddenly, got a better job with a California firm, and the fellow who took over didn't like my innovative approach. He assigned a reviewer who obviously deferred to his point of view. Gradually, this new editor along with the reviewer turned the whole thing around so that it looked nothing like what it started out as. It was a totally different book. And it wasn't the book I wanted to do, either."

Editors and authors have plenty of horror stories to tell about joint authorship projects. This seems to be another constant problem, with coauthors as likely to fight as husbands and wives, sometimes staying together in a tense relationship only "for the sake of the book."

"These two lawyers," one editor explained, "began a book for us on business law. They were friends and were teaching together at a community college. About six months into the project, one of the lawyers ran off with the other one's wife. Well, you can imagine the bad vibes between them. But neither wanted to bow out of the project, both insisting that they were making the major contribution. Since there had been a considerable advance involved, we weren't too eager to drop it. The contract of course doesn't allow for dropping a book because of adultery. But, tell me, how do you get two people to work cooperatively under those circumstances?"

This situation is, of course, not the norm. More typically, as the book develops, trouble crops up in three areas between coauthors. First, there may be perceptible differences in their relative abilities, both stylistic and content-related. The early reviewers may even identify one of the coauthors as a liability to the project. I once reviewed a book where half the chapter were beautifully crafted and cleverly executed, but the other half were almost illiterate and ineffably dull. I knew at once two authors were at work on the project, and that they should never have been paired together. When this happens, and it is pointed out, it can produce an awkward situation when the less-qualified author may be asked to bow out of the project, and feelings can certainly be bruised under those circumstances.

A second problem with a joint-authorship project, be it article-length or book-length, is that it doubles the likelihood of procrastination or delay. Invariably, one of the authors undergoes an illness (physical or mental), loses a loved one, travels to Kathmandu on sabbatical, loses his briefcase with all his notes, develops a writer's block, becomes an alcoholic—or all of the above. "I'm sorry the book will be delayed," the other author explains, "but my coauthor. . . ." The more authors involved in a project, the greater this difficulty becomes.

The third problem is that two equally competent coauthors may be writing two excellent but different books simultaneously. Each, working independently, goes into the project with his or her own ideas of what the book is about, and what its underlying philosophy will be. Only when they piece together their individual chapters into a whole book does it become clear that there is no consistent point of view among the chapters; that the book does not hold together.

All these problems can be avoided, editors and authors agree, when there is planning at the beginning, and communication and review of each other's work along the way. The editor should take a forceful hand in keeping on top of multiple-authorship projects to ensure that they don't run into these problems.

What makes a book successful? Why does one book do so much better than another? At what point can a publisher or author predict with some accuracy how successful a project will be?

"Of course you can't know at the beginning if a project will succeed or not," one editor explained, "or else we would only be signing successful projects. But there are certain things to look for. I personally pay special attention to the author's attitude and track record, if there is one. How does the author respond to criticism about his work? I've had people who handed in material with real potential, but the minute I started making suggestions, they became adamant. They didn't want to change a word. I know that books aren't developed that way. You have to have an open mind."

Another editor suggested that 80% of what makes a book successful is the marketing and sales effort by the publisher. "Sure, you have to start with a decent product," she explained, "but how it's handled in-house makes a big difference in how it sells. Do you have a strong editor behind you—someone who has the ear of the executives upstairs? Is the publisher very committed to that project or are they scatter-shooting; that is, bringing out lots of books in one area and hoping that any one of them will sell? Does the publisher have a track record in marketing this type of material?"

Another piece of advice came from a successful author who had published many magazine articles, several contributed chapters, and three full-length books. A psychologist, he articulated a position that I have personally found helpful over the years. "I think the expectations with which one goes into a project affect how you feel about its outcome. First of all there is the self-fulfilling prophesy. If you expect to perform well, if you expect to produce a good book or article, you are more likely to do so. Likewise, if you expect to fail, or to produce something mediocre, you are more likely to bring that upon yourself."

Then there is the self-defeating tendency to create disappointment by having unrealistic expectations. If you are doing a book that can realistically be expected to sell 10,000 copies, but you are hoping against hope that it will sell 50,000, even if it sells double what it is expected to sell you will still be disappointed because it didn't sell the unreasonably high amount you set up for it. Some people continually create expectations that disappoint them.

APPENDIX A

Preparing Your Manuscript

The physical presentation of your manuscript, whether it is an article, book proposal, or completed book manuscript, is important in making a proper impression on the person who will read it as well as assuring a quick turnaround into production after the final copy is submitted. The inclusion with the manuscript of what is often called the "production package" will avoid lengthy delays. This package includes permissions forms, art work, and front and end matter (preface, appendix). Each periodical and publishing house has its own specific guidelines. These should be consulted before submitting your material. In this appendix, I have tried out outline what are generally considered the standards for manuscript preparation, based on *A Guide for Wiley Authors* (New York: John Wiley & Sons, 1980).

Physical Presentation

Use white, nonerasable twenty- or twenty-four-pound bond paper, 8½ by 11 inches. Never use onion skin or specially treated chemical papers because they tend to smudge. Type on one side of the page only. Leave at least 1½-inch margins on all sides. Start chapter titles 1½ inches from the top of the page. The space is needed for editing the manuscript, typemarking it, and placing queries. Use a good black ribbon. If your typewriter can use a carbon ribbon, use one. If not, change the fabric ribbon and clean the typefaces frequently to ensure a clear impression. Double-space or triple-space the entire manuscript, including the text, quoted material, footnotes, references, lists, tables, legends (or figure captions), appendixes, and glossaries. Leave triple space between displayed mathematical equations and chemical reactions as well as above and below heads, lists, quotations, footnotes, and other special material.

Page Numbering

Number manuscript pages consecutively with a single number (1, 2, 3; not 1-1, 1-2, 1-3) beginning with page 1 for the first page of Chapter 1 (or Part 1) and continuing through all appendixes and other back matter, such as references and bibliography. Place the number in the upper right corner of the page. Include tables in the numbering sequence. Do not include illustrations, figure captions, or front matter.

Headings

A well-wrought article or chapter is usually divided into subordinate sections by headings. Headings are useful for two reasons: they assist the writer in organizing the article by grouping related paragraphs into idea units. They also highlight the logic of the article by showing subordinate relationships among the parts.

Different publishers have their own rules about headings, although virtually all of them recognize what are called A heads, B heads, and C heads. It is best to use only two levels or three levels of headings, although certain occasions will require a fourth-level heading. A generally accepted format, although not universal, is as follows:

NUMBER 1: "A" HEAD GOES HERE
The "A" head is centered, and all of the letters are capitalized.

Number 2: "B" Head Goes Here
The "B" head is centered and underlined. The main words begin with capital letters.

Number 3: "C" Head Goes Here
The "C" head is typed flush left on a separate line. The main word begin with capital letters.

Always type levels of headings consistently and distinguish clearly among them (either by typing them as above, or by placing encircled Arabic numbers in the margins: (1), (2), (3). Leave triple space above and below each subhead.

Tables

Type all tables double spaced, including title, column headings, rules, and footnotes. Type each table on a separate page. Type or draw a rule (as wide as the table) above table column heads, below column heads, and below the table (above any table footnotes). Add short rules when needed to bring together several column headings under one major heading. Do not use vertical rules. Do not use leaders (dots) between columns. Do not break words. Do not abbreviate words merely to fit them in. Indent subitems in the left column. See page 127 for an example of a typset table that follows these directions. Place each table following the manuscript page on which it is mentioned and include it when numbering the manuscript pages.

Lists, too, are typed double-spaced. Leave triple-space above and below a list. Type and number all lists in the same way throughout the manuscript.

Quotations and References

A quotation of less than three lines is typed within the body of text, set off by quotation marks. Quotations of three lines or more are block indented with 5 extra spaces on the left margin and typed double-spaced. They do not use quotation marks unless such marks are included in the quoted material. Leave triple-space above and below indented quotations.

References are also typed double-spaced, with three lines of space left between each reference. Keep references in strict alphabetical or numerical order. The reference format will be based on the conventions of your discipline. For example, this book could appear in either of these two widely-used forms, depending on the publication.

Belkin, G.S. *Getting published: A guide for business people and other professionals.* New York: John Wiley & Sons, 1983.

– or –

1983   Belkin, Gary S.   *Getting published: A guide for business people and other professionals.* (New York: John Wiley & Sons).

Type all references throughout the manuscript in the same form and sequence. In certain fields, such as education and psychology, the standard reference format differs from the more widely used format most of us learned in school. The best way to be sure of which to use is to thumb through a recent issue of the periodical to which you are sending the article. That way you will find the format they prefer for book and article citations.

Illustrations

Keep the illustrations separate from the manuscript and the legends. Do not include them when numbering pages of the manuscript. Do not insert blank sheets or photocopies of illustrations within the manuscript. Cite figure numbers in your text discussion in sequence; the editor will then know where to place the figures.

Legends or captions should be included with the illustrations. They should be clearly numbered to correspond to the illustration to which they pertain. If there are less than five, you can place them on the page with the illustration if that is possible. Otherwise, prepare a separate legend list.

Equations

In many fields, such as the sciences, medicine, mathematics, business, teaching, and communications, equations are important in articles or books. Because equations demand exactitude it is important to clearly indicate them on the manuscript to minimize the chances of error occurring as the manuscript is set into galley.

General Rules. Leave three lines of space between displayed equations and four lines above and below a set of equations. Center equations on the page, with the equation number, if there is one, in parentheses at the right margin of the page. Break multiline equations before plus (+), minus (–), or equal (=) signs.

Signs, Symbols and Special Alphabets. Type all of the signs, symbols, and letters that you can. Write in all others, adding marginal clarification where required. If your typewriter does not have a degree sign (°), type it as a lowercase o. If your typewriter does not have a zero, type a capital O; never use a lowercase o for zero, even in subscripts and superscripts. Identify special type letters in this way.

Boldface (wiggly underline):

Italic type (underline):

Small capitals (double underline):

Script letter (circle):

German gothic letter (square):

Sans serif letter (triangle):

Handwritten symbols and any special-alphabet or Greek letters should be identified in the manuscript the first time they occur. In quoting from technical articles or books, follow the copy precisely in typing capital or lowercase letters; they have mathematical significance.

Alignment. Maintain the correct alignment between parts of equations. Center the plus (+), minus (–), times (x), and equal (=) signs against the expressions to which they apply. Type subscripts and superscripts half a line below or above the symbols they qualify.

Spacing. Leave space before and after expressions such as cos, sin, log, In, exp, Re, and Im. Leave space before and after the plus, minus, times, and equal signs (and other signs of operation) except in subscripts and superscripts.

Fractions. In the text, type fractions in shilling form: *a/b*. In displayed equations, type them in bar form:

$$\frac{a}{b}$$

Accents
Type or write in, precisely and consistently, any diacritical mark.

(é)	acute accent
(è)	grave accent
(ô)	circumflex
(ñ)	tilde
(ō)	macron
(ŭ)	breve
(č)	hacek
(oö)	diaeresis (or umlaut)
(ç)	cedilla

Front Matter
Type all of the front matter material (title page, author list, preface, and contents) double-spaced. Number the pages separately from the text manuscript. The table of contents should include part titles, chapter titles, and one or two levels of heads. Distinguish a lower-level head by indenting it.

Permissions

It is your responsiblity as an author to obtain written permission for the use of any material that is not your own. You should write for permission as soon as your decide to use this material. You may later decide to delete it, even after permission has been granted, but as a courtesy you should inform the copyright owner.

Material that is not protected by copyright belongs to the community at large; it is in the public domain, and permission to use it is not required. Public domain material includes most government publications, tables that contain generally known information (for example, units of measure), and text material such as quoted passages from Shakespeare or anything else where the copyright has expired. However, government publications may contain copyrighted material that was used with the permission of the copyright owner; publication in a government document does not authorize use of the material without the consent of the copyright owner.

When Permission is Needed. There are three kinds of borrowed material – text, tables, and illustrations (line drawings, and halftones) – and the simple acknowledgment of the source in your manuscript cannot substitute for formal permission. Although there are no absolute rules concerning the length of a borrowed quotation or the extent to which a borrowed illustration must be changed to become original, according to accepted guidelines you would probably do best to obtain permission in the following cases.

- Prose quotations of 400 words or more from a full-length book (either a single quotation or several shorter quotations from a single work).
- Any portion of a play, a poem, or a song.
- A table, diagram, or illustration (including cartoons, photographs, or maps) that you are reproducing exactly or adapting slightly. The mere redrawing of an illustration is not enough to make it an original drawing. There must be substantial additions that are themselves capable of being copyrighted. Even when there are conceptual additions, you must obtain permission to make a new version of the table or illustration that you have used as a basis for your own.

Some authors go overboard and request permission for every little quote they use. This is not only unnecessary but expensive, since each permission costs a fee which is eventually deducted from the author's royalty account. If in doubt, consult the author's guide provided by your publisher to see what their specific permission requirements are.

How to Obtain Permission. Use the permission request form on page 155. Write a follow-up letter or telephone the copyright owner if you have had no reply within three or four weeks. The fees charged for reprinting copyrighted material must be agreed on, in each case, by the seller and the buyer of the rights. Most publishers have standard rates for various classes of books, but there are no generally accepted rates for all publishers. Whenever the rates seem unusually high or require a pro rata share of your royalties, you are probably best off eliminating this material from your manuscript.

Sample Permission Request Letter

Date Sent:

Dear Permissions Editor:

I am preparing a book in psychology to be published by the college text book division of John Wiley & Sons, Inc. of New York on or about November, 1985. We plan a book of about 400 pages, intended for the college market. May I have your permission to use the following material in this and future editions and revisions of this book:

We will, of course, cite a standard source line. If you have any specific credit line requirements, please make them known in the space below. These rights will in no way restrict republication of your material by you or by others authorized by you. Should you not control these rights in their entirety, would you kindly let me know to whom I must write.

I would appreciate your consent to this request. For your convenience, a release form is provided below, and a copy of this letter is enclosed for your files.

Sincerely,

Gary S. Belkin, Ed.D.
Assistant Professor of Counseling
Long Island University

RELEASE FORM

Permission Granted, signature   Title   Date

APPENDIX **B**

Where to Send Your Material

This appendix will offer publication opportunities for magazine articles or full-length books, both popular (trade), text, and technical/scholarly. Each publication is numbered and indexed in a comprehensive occupation index at the end of the appendix. This will help you locate your best opportunities.

These publishers have generally been receptive to reviewing and publishing the works of new writers when their material meets the standards of the publication. All of them will accept unsolicited material if it is sent in the appropriate form and includes a self-addressed, stamped envelope for its return upon refusal. I suggest you contact an editor of the magazine or publishing house before sending your material to see that it gets to the right person and to see if your project fits in with the general kinds of things they publish. In the case of magazines, you should look over the most recent issue before getting in touch with the editor.

The list of magazines is organized first by some major subject areas, followed by a list of ungrouped publications. More comprehensive coverage can be found in the reference books discussed in chapter 4. Following the list of magazines is a list of book publishers. At the end of the appendix is a list of occupations and some suggested publication possibilities for individuals writing in each of those areas.

Magazines

Arts and Antiques

1. American Antiques
   Lindecroft Publications, Inc.
   RD 1 Box 241
   New Hope, PA 18938

2. The Antiques Journal
   Babka Publishing Co.
   100 Bryant Street
   Dubuque, Iowa 52001

3. Antiques World
   Antiques News Association
   122 East 42nd Street
   New York, NY 10017

Advertising and Marketing

4. Advertising Age
   220 E 42nd Street
   New York, NY 10017

5. Industrial Marketing
   Crain Communications, Inc.
   708 Third Avenue
   New York, NY 10017

6. Madison Avenue Magazine
   369 Lexington Avenue
   New York, NY 10017

7. Market Motivation News
   411 A. Newport Way
   Jamesburg, NJ 08831

8. Marketing Times
   Sales and Marketing Executives International, Inc.
   380 Lexington Avenue
   New York, NY 10017

Aeronautics and Aviation

9. General Aviation News
   Box 1416
   Winston Field
   Snyder, TX 79549

10. Invitation to Flying
    Ziff-Davis Publishing Co.
    1 Park Avenue
    New York, NY 10016

11. Journal of Airport Management
    Amer. Assoc. of Airport Executives
    2029 K Street, NW
    Washington, DC 20006

Business, Banking and Finance

12. Administrative Management
    Geyer-McAllister Publications, Inc.
    51 Madison Avenue
    New York, NY 10010

13. Financial Analysts Journal
    Financial Analysts Federation
    1633 Broadway, 14th Floor
    New York, NY 10019

14. Forbes
    50 Fifth Avenue
    New York, NY 10011

15. Fortune Magazine
    1271 Avenue of the Americas
    New York, NY 10020

16. In Business
    JG Press
    Box 323
    Emmaus, PA 18049

17. Income Opportunities
    Davis Publications
    380 Lexington Avenue
    New York, NY 10017

18. Industry Magazine
    Associated Industries of Massachusetts
    4005 Prudential Tower
    Boston, MA 02199

19. Nation's Business
    Chamber of Commerce of the United States
    1615 H Street NW
    Washington, DC 20062

Conservation and Ecology

20. Environmental Law
    American Bar Association
    1800 M Street NW
    Washington, DC 20036

21. Geojourney
    Florida Conservation News
    Florida Department of Natural Resources
    1300 Commonwealth Boulevard
    Tallahassee, FL 32303

22. Iowa Conservationist
    300 4th Street
    Des Moines, IA 50319

23. Journal of Environmental Health
    National Environmental Health Association
    1200 Lincoln Street
    Denver, CO 80203

24. Journal of Environmental Management
    Academic Press, Inc.
    111 Fifth Avenue
    New York, NY 10003

Economics

25. Engineering Economist
    American Institute of Industrial Engineers
    25 Technology Park/Atlanta
    Norcross, GA 30092

26. Journal of Economic Issues
    Association for Evolutionary Economics
    509 Bus. Adm. Bldg.
    The Pennsylvania State University
    University Park, PA 16802

Education

27. American Teacher
    The American Federation of Teachers
    11 DuPont Circle, NW
    Washington, DC 20036

28. Journal of Business Education
    4000 Albemarle Street, NW
    Washington, DC 20016

29. Journal of Developmental and Remedial Education
    Appalachian State University
    Boone, NC 28608

30. Journal of Economic Education
    Joint Council on Economic Education
    1212 Avenue of the Americas
    New York, NY 10036

31. School Arts
    50 Portland Street
    Worcester, MA 01608

Engineering, Science, Technology

32. Broadcast Engineering
    Box 12901
    Overland Park, KS 66212

33. Civil Engineering
    American Society of Civil Engineers
    345 East 47th Street
    New York, NY 10017

34. Electronics Today International
    25 Overlea Boulevard
    Toronto, Ontario Canada M4H 1B1

35. Mechanix Illustrated
    1515 Broadway
    New York, NY 10036

36. Omni
    909 Third Avenue
    New York, NY 10022

37. Popular Electronics
    1 Park Avenue
    New York, NY 10016

38. Recording Engineer/Producer
    Box 2449
    Hollywood, CA 90028

Food

39. Fine Dining
    Connell Publications
    7300 Biscayne Boulevard
    Suite 333
    Miami, FL 33138

40. Food Management
    Harcourt Brace Jovanovich
    757 Third Avenue
    New York, NY 10017

Health

41. Alternatives
    Box 486
    New Market, VA 22844

42. American Industrial Hygiene Association Journal
    475 Wolf Ledges Parkway
    Akron, OH 44311

43. American Journal of Public Health
    American Public Health Association
    1015 15th Street, NW
    Washington, DC 20005

44. Journal of Community Health
    Human Sciences Press
    72 Fifth Avenue
    New York, NY 10011

45. Journal of School Health
    American School Health Association
    PO Box 708
    Kent, OH 44240

Hospital Management

46. Hospital Supervisor's Bulletin
    Bureau of Business Practice
    24 Rope Ferry Road
    Waterford, CT 06385

47. Hospital Week
    American Hospital Association
    840 No. Lake Shore Drive
    Chicago, IL 60611

48. Hospitals
    American Hospital Publishing, Inc.
    211 E Chicago Avenue
    Chicago, IL 60611

Insurance

49. Business Insurance
    740 N Rush Street
    Chicago, IL 60611

Journalism and Writing

50. Columbia Journalism Review
    700 Journalism Building
    Columbia University
    New York, NY 10027

51. Editor & Publisher
    575 Lexington Avenue
    New York, NY 10022

52. The Writer
    8 Arlington Street
    Boston, MA 02116

53. Writer's Digest
    9933 Alliance Road
    Cincinnati, OH 45242

Law

54. American Barrister
    American Bar Association
    1155 E 60th Street
    Chicago, IL 60637

55. Student Lawyer
    American Bar Association
    1155 E 60th Street
    Chicago, IL 60637

Library Science

56. American Libraries
    50 E Huron Street
    Chicago, IL 60611

57. Library Journal
    1180 Avenue of the Americas
    New York, NY 10036

58. School Library Journal
    1180 Avenue of the Americas
    New York, NY 10036

Management, Sales and Training

59. Manage
    2210 Arbor Boulevard
    Dayton, OH 45439

60. Sales and Marketing Management
    633 Third Avenue
    New York, NY 10017

61. Sales Manager's Bulletin
    The Bureau of Business Practice
    24 Rope Ferry Road
    Waterford, CT 06386

62. Salesman's Opportunity
    Opportunity Press, Inc.
    6 N Michigan Avenue
    Chicago, IL 60602

63. Training
    731 Hennepin Ave.
    Minneapolis, MN 55403

Medicine, Dentistry, Nursing

64. American Journal of Nursing
    555 W 57th Street
    New York, NY 10019

65. Dental Economics
    PennWell Publishing Co.
    P.O. Box 1260
    1421 S Sheridan Road
    Tulsa, OK 74101

66. Dental Hygiene
    American Dental Hygienists Association
    444 N Michigan Avenue
    Chicago, IL 60611

67. Journal of Nursing Care
    265 Post Road W.
    Westport, CT 06880

68. Journal of Practical Nursing
    254 W. 31st Street
    New York, NY 10001

69. Medical Care
    J.B. Lippincott Co., Publishers
    East Washington Square
    Philadelphia, PA 19105

70. New Dentist
    211 E. Chicago Avenue
    Chicago, IL 60611

Military

71. Army Magazine
    2425 Wilson Boulevard
    Arlington, VA 22201

72. Marine Corps Gazette
    P.O. Box 1775
    Quantico, VA 22134

73. The Retired Officer
    201 N Washington Street
    Alexandria, VA 22314

Religion

74. Baptist History and Heritage
    127 Ninth Avenue N.
    Nashville, TN 37234

75. Christian Herald
    40 Overlook Drive
    Chappaqua, NY 10514

76. Judaism: A Quarterly Journal
    American Jewish Congress
    15 E 84th Street
    New York, NY 10028

77. Lutheran Forum
    308 W 46th Street
    New York, NY 10036

Urban Planning and Public Policy

78. Planning and Public Policy
    University of Illinois at Urbana-Champaign
    909 W Nevada Street
    Urbana, IL 61801

79. Public Administration Review
    1225 Connecticut Avenue
    Washington, DC 20036

80. Urban Affairs Quarterly
    275 S. Beverly Drive
    Beverly Hills, CA 90212

Miscellaneous

81. Bartender
    Box 707
    Livingston, NJ 07039

82. Bon Appetit
    5900 Wilshire Boulevard
    Los Angeles, CA 90036

83. Commodities Magazine
    219 Parkade
    Cedar Falls, IA 50613

84. Computerworld
    375 Cochituate Road
    Box 880
    Framingham, MA 01701

85. Corrections
    116 W 32nd Street
    New York, NY 10001

86. Financial Executive
    633 Third Avenue
    New York, NY 10017

87. High Fidelity
    825 Seventh Avenue
    New York, NY 10019

88. Home Energy Digest
    8009 34th Avenue S.
    Minneapolis, MN 55420

89. Modern Office Procedures
    1111 Chester Avenue
    Cleveland, OH 44114

90. Museum Magazine
    260 Madison Avenue
    New York, NY 10016

91. Personal Computing
    50 Essex Street
    Rochelle Park, NJ 07662

9   Personnel and Guidance Journal
    5203 Leesburg Pike
    Falls Church, VA 22041

93. Progressive Architecture
    600 Summer Street
    Stamford, CT 06904

94. Retailer and Marketing News
    Box 57194
    Dallas, TX 75207

95. Solar Age
    American Solar Energy Society
    Church Hill
    Harrissville, NH 03450

96. Workbench
    4251 Pennsylvania Avenue
    Kansas City, MO 64111

Book Publishers

97. Harry N. Abrams, Inc.
    110 E 59th Street
    New York, NY 10022

98. Academic Press, Inc.
    111 Fifth Avenue
    New York, NY 10003

99. Addison-Wesley Publishing Co., Inc.
    Reading, MA 01867

100. Allen & Unwin, Inc.
     9 Winchester Terrace
     Winchester, MA 01890

101. Allyn & Bacon, Inc.
     470 Atlantic Avenue
     Boston, MA 02210
     or
     7 Wells Avenue
     Newton, MA 02159

102. Avery Publishing Group, Inc.
     89 Baldwin Terrace
     Wayne, NJ 07470

103. Ballinger Publishing Co.
     54 Church Street
     Harvard Square
     Cambridge, MA 02138

104. A.S. Barnes & Co., Inc.
     11175 Flinkote Avenue
     San Diego, CA 92121

105. Beacon Press
     25 Beacon Street
     Boston, MA 02018

106. Better Homes and Gardens Books
     17 & Locust Streets
     Des Moines, IO 50336

107. BNA Books (Bureau of National Affairs, Inc.)
     1231 25th Street NW
     Washington, DC 20037

108. Butterworth Publishers
     10 Tower Office Park
     Woburn, MA 01801

109. Cambridge University Press
     32 E 57th Street
     New York, NY 10022

110. Career Publishing, Inc.
     931 N Main Street
     Box 5486
     Orange, CA 92667

111. CBI Publishing Co., Inc.
     51 Sleeper Street
     Boston, MA 02210

112. Chilton Book Co.
     Chilton Way
     Radnor, PA 19089

113. Citadel Press
     120 Enterprise Avenue
     Secaucus, NJ 07094

114. Contemporary Books
     180 N. Michigan Avenue
     Chicago, IL 60601

115. Coward-McCann
     200 Madison Avenue
     New York, NY 10016

116. Creative Books Co.
     8210 Varna Avenue
     Van Nuys, CA 91402

117. Delmar Publishers, Inc.
     50 Wolf Road
     Albany, NY 12205

118. T.S. Denison & Co., Inc.
     9601 Newton Avenue S
     Minneapolis, MN 55431

119. Dilithium Press
     11000 SW 11th Street
     Beaverton, OR 97005

120. Doubleday & Co., Inc.
     245 Park Avenue
     New York, NY 10167

121. Edits Publishers
     Box 7234
     San Diego, CA 92107

122. Elsevier/Nelson Books
     Two Park Avenue
     New York, NY 10016

123. Everest House, Publishers
     33 W 60th Street
     New York, NY 10023

124. Frederick Fell Publishers, Inc.
     386 Park Avenue S
     New York, NY 10016

125. Garland Publishing, Inc.
     136 Madison Avenue
     New York, NY 10016

126. Goodyear Publishing Co., Inc.
     1640 5th Street
     Santa Monica, CA 90401

127. Gordon Press Publishers
     Box 459
     Bowling Green Station
     New York, NY 10004

128. Grossett and Dunlap, Inc.
     200 Madison Avenue
     New York, NY 10010

129. Harcourt Brace Jovanovich
757 Third Avenue
New York, NY 10017

130. Harper & Row, Publishers, Inc.
10 E 53rd Street
New York, NY 10022

131. Hart Publishing Co., Inc.
12 E 12th Street
New York, NY 10003

132. Hayden Book Co., Inc.
50 Essex Street
Rochelle Park, NJ 07662

133. D.C. Heath & Co.
125 Spring Street
Lexington, MA 02173

134. Hill & Wang
19 Union Square W.
New York, NY 10003

135. Holmes & Meier Publishers, Inc.
30 Irving Place
New York, NY 10003

136. Holt, Rinehart & Winston
521 Fifth Avenue
New York, NY 10175

137. Horizon Press
156 Fifth Avenue
New York, NY 10010

138. Houghton Mifflin Co.
1 Beacon Street
Boston, MA 02108

139. Human Sciences Press, Inc.
72 Fifth Avenue
New York, NY 10011

140. International Marine Publishing Co.
     21 Elm Street
     Camden, ME 04843

141. The Interstate Printers & Publishers, Inc.
     Box 594
     19 N Jackson Street
     Danville, IL 61832

142. JAI Press, Inc.
     36 Sherwood Place
     P.O. Box 1678
     Greenwich, CT 06830

143. Jossey-Bass, Inc., Publishers
     433 California Street
     San Francisco, CA 94104

144. Kern Publications,
     Data Dynamics, Inc.
     190 Duck Hill Road, Box 1029
     Duxbury, MA 02332

145. Lane and Associates, Inc.
     P.O. Box 3063
     La Jolla, CA 92038

146. Law-Arts Publishers
     453 Greenwich Street
     New York, NY 10013

147. Libra Publishers, Inc.
     391 Willets Road
     Rosyln Heights, NY 11577

148. Little, Brown & Co.
     34 Beacon Street
     Boston, MA 02106

149. Lothrop, Lee & Shepard Books
     105 Madison Avenue
     New York, NY 10016

150. McGraw-Hill Book Co.
     1221 Avenue of the Americas
     New York, NY 10020

151. Macmillan Publishing Co., Inc.
     866 Third Avenue
     New York, NY 10022

152. Charles E. Merrill Publishing Co.
     1300 Alum Creek Drive
     Columbus, OH 43216

153. The MIT Press
     28 Carleton Street
     Cambridge, MA 02142

154. William Morrow & Co., Inc.
     105 Madison Avenue
     New York, NY 10016

155. National Book Co.
     333 SW Park Avenue
     Portland, OR 97205

156. Nelson-Hall Publishers
     111 N Canal Street
     Chicago, IL 60606

157. R&R Newkirk,
     ITT Publishing
     Box 1727
     Indianapolis, IN 46036

158. Nichols Publishing Co.
     Box 96
     New York, NY 10024

159. Noyes Data Corp.
     Mill Road & Grand Avenue
     Park Ridge, NJ 07656

160. Ohio State University Press
     Neilwood Gables
     2088 Neil Avenue
     Columbus, OH 43210

161. 101 Productions
     834 Mission Street
     San Francisco, CA 94103

162. Paladin Press
     Box 1307
     Boulder, CO 80306

163. Pilot Books
     347 Fifth Avenue
     New York, NY 10016

164. Platt & Munk
     51 Madison Avenue
     New York, NY 10010

165. Plenum Publishing Corp.
     233 Spring Street
     New York, NY 10013

166. Porter Sargent Publishers, Inc.
     11 Beacon Street
     Boston, MA 12108

167. Clarkson N. Potter, Inc.
     1 Park Avenue
     New York, NY 10016

168. Praeger Publishers
     521 Fifth Avenue
     New York, NY 10175

169. Prentice-Hall, Inc.
     Englewood Cliffs, NJ 07632

170. Putnam Publishing Group
     200 Madison Avenue
     New York, NY 10016

171. Quartet Books, Inc.
     360 Park Avenue S
     New York, NY 10010

172. R & E Research Associates, Inc.
     936 Industrial Avenue
     Palo Alto, CA 94303

173. Random House, Inc.
     201 E 50th Street
     New York, NY 10022

174. Realtors National Marketing Institute
     430 N Michigan Avenue
     Chicago, IL 60611

175. Reston Publishing Co., Inc.
     11480 Sunset Hills Road
     Reston, VA 22090

176. St. Martin's Press, Inc.
     175 Fifth Avenue
     New York, NY 10010

177. Schenkman Publishing Co., Inc.
     331 Broadway
     Cambridge, MA 02139

178. Science Books International
     51 Sleeper Street
     Boston, MA 02110

179. Schocken Books, Inc.
     200 Madison Avenue
     New York, NY 10016

180. Scholarly Resources, Inc.
     104 Greenhill Avenue
     Wilmington, DE 19805

181. The Shoe String Press, Inc.
     Box 4327
     995 Sherman Avenue
     Hamden, CT 06514

182. Slack, Inc.
     6900 Grove Road
     Thorofare, NJ 08086

183. Robert Speller & Sons, Publishers, Inc.
     30 E 23rd Street
     New York, NY 10010

184. Stackpole Books
     Box 1831
     Harrisburg, PA 17105

185. Sterling Publishing Co., Inc.
     2 Park Avenue
     New York, NY 10016

186. Structures Publishing Company
     Ideals Publishing Corp.
     11315 Watertown Plank Road
     Milwaukee, WI 53226

187. Sybex, Inc.
     2344 Sixth Street
     Berkeley, CA 94710

188. TAB Books, Inc.
     Blue Ridge
     Summit, PA 17214

189. Taplinger Publishing Co., Inc.
     132 W 22nd Street
     New York, NY 10011

190. J.P. Tarcher, Inc.
     9110 Sunset Boulevard
     Los Angeles, CA 90069

191. Temple University Press
     Broad & Oxford Streets
     Philadelphia, PA 19122

192. Ten Speed Press
     Box 7123
     Berkeley, CA 94707

193. Transaction Books
     Rutgers University
     New Brunswick, NJ 08903

194. University Associates, Inc.
     Box 26240
     8517 Production Avenue
     San Diego, CA 92126

195. University of Pennsylvania Press
     3933 Walnut Street
     Philadelphia, PA 19104

196. VGM Career Horizons
     (Division of National Textbook Co.)
     8529 Niles Center Road
     Skokie, IL 60077

197. Wadsworth Publishing Co.
     10 Davis Drive
     Belmont, CA 94002

198. Weber Systems, Inc.
     8437 Mayfield Road
     Chesterland, OH 44021

199. West Publishing Co.
     Box 3526
     50 W. Kellogg Boulevard
     St. Paul, MN 55165

200. Westview Press, Inc.
     5500 Central Avenue
     Boulder, CO 80301

201. John Wiley & Sons, Inc.
     605 Third Avenue
     New York, NY 10158

Index By Occupations

The most appropriate magazine or book publisher for *your* article or book can only be determined after carefully examining all the appropriate sources, as outlined in Chapter 4. Below are a few suggestions to consider at the outset. The numbers refer to the list of publication possibilities in this chapter. Next to each occupation are those magazines and book publishers that have brought out articles for books in that area or have expressed an interest in this or related areas. You might give these your first priority, if your article appears to fit into the framework of these publications.

179

Index